Open Boxes

the gifts of living a full and connected life

Christine Organ

Open Boxes

the gifts of living a full and connected life

Christine Organ

220 Publishing

Chicago, Illinois
220 Publishing
(A Division of 220 Communications)

Published by 220 Publishing
(A Division of 220 Communications)

PO Box 8186
Chicago, IL 60680-8186

www.220communications.com
www.twitter.com/220comm

For more information on the author, visit:
www.christineorgan.com

Cover and Interior Design by Julie M. Holloway of JMHCre8ive.com

Cover image: © grki - Fotolia.com

ISBN 9 78-1-634-52366-0
Printed in the USA

For Matthew, Jackson, and Teddy

You are, indeed, my miracles

Table of Contents

Everyday Miracles

Introduction

"Invisible threads are the strongest ties."
—Friedrich Nietzsche

The closet in the upstairs hallway of our small Georgian house is lined with boxes. Some of the boxes are pale blue plastic, making the contents easily identifiable. Others are made of thick cardboard, decorated in flamboyant floral patterns, bright polka dots, or soft pastel paisleys. The boxes' contents are as different as their exteriors—some of the boxes are filled with family photos, some with old report cards and elementary school projects from decades ago, and others with softly worn love letters written between my husband and me over the course of our relationship.

Stacked neatly, one on top of the other like a patchwork quilt, the boxes create some semblance of order, concealing the hodgepodge collection of memories and jumbled mess of mementos, tattered papers, and faded photos scattered inside. They separate, contain, and hide the relative disorder that lies buried inside. I love the boxes for this. The organization, order, separation, and concealment . . . honestly, it's enough to make a (recovering) Type A perfectionist like myself almost squeal with delight.

The trouble is, while boxes are great in our closets, offices, attics, and basements, keeping boxes isn't all that helpful for creating meaningful connection, finding spiritual fulfillment, or living a full—a busting-at-the-seams full—life. When we box up our lives, we set boundaries and draw clear lines, hiding vulnerabilities, isolating spiritual practices from our daily routine, and separating family from career from faith. Box-keeping doesn't work all that well for those of us who want a life of meaning, purpose, and joy. While these tiny little boxes—with their neat rows and pretty exteriors—might give the illusion of order and put-together-ness, they also hide all the messy goodness inside.

When we live in this fragmented and disjointed world, with all of these box-like compartments for each facet of our lives, the spiritual is cordoned off from the secular. We keep our work life separate from our home life, which is detached from our social circles that are, in turn, kept a safe distance from our spiritual community. Yet despite these disjointed compartments and the frayed edges jumbled up inside the boxes, we have an inherent, almost primal, need to feel connected in a meaningful way to ourselves, to others, to our communities, to God, and to something bigger and greater than the separate aspects of our day-to-day lives. We have a deep yearning to feel a part of something more significant than the daily chaos and more meaningful than the monotony of our daily routines.

Like Caroline Myss wrote, "We're on this planet to learn to be spiritual beings in a physical body, to gain consciousness of our greater purpose."[1] As a result, we realize a constant urge to break open the boxes and toss the contents into one big heap, letting the love letters and school reports mingle with the family vacation photos and baptismal gowns. Despite our tidy rows of boxes separating this from that, we hold a quiet hope for sacred connection; a tiny voice wonders if there might be some kind of divine undercurrent running through it all. We want to throw the contents of our tidy boxes together, with some faith that the pieces can be tied together, but we're afraid of what might happen if some of the pieces get lost in the shuffle.

So we separate. We package. And we hide.

---

[1] Caroline Myss, *Invisible Acts of Power*, (New York: Free Press, 2006), 3.

The world can be a drab, disheartening, and downright nasty place at times. It's no surprise that we find it easier to simply separate ourselves with our pretty boxes, stuffing our hopes and fears into plastic flip-top receptacles. Just a half-hour of the evening news, for example, bombards us with stories of school shootings and gang violence, bombs and explosions, poverty and nuclear weapons, and all those things that don't make sense. It's far better, we rationalize, to stuff all this horror into one of the boxes before the salt can dry on our tear-stained cheeks. Even the happiness and joy—babies with wiggly toes, job promotions, and first "I love you's"—get stuffed into their own boxes, a lid tightly placed on top lest the joy escape or dissipate.

We separate. We package. We hide.

And yet while we are separating, packaging, and hiding, there's this raspy voice coming from somewhere deep inside, asking: *Could there be a way to tie this all together, a way to make sense of all this madness and chaos, all this goodness and cruelty?* The question might come when we're sitting in church, head bowed. Or it might be found at the bottom of a bottle of wine. Or it might appear when we look into our children's inquisitive eyes. But it arises eventually.

The questioning voice reached a fever pitch for me about seven or eight years ago. By all accounts, my life was full and satisfying. I had a handful of good friends and enough acquaintances to maintain an active social life. My husband and I had a stable and loving relationship. A new baby filled my days with diapers to be changed, smiles to be photographed, and bottles to be prepared. Our families were supportive and engaged with our lives. I went to church periodically, prayed every now and then, and read books by Eckhart Tolle and Anne Lamott to fill the gaps. And after a fairly successful career in the legal industry, I felt satisfied and ready to move into the new role of stay-at-home mom.

On paper, everything seemed to add up to a "good life." Yet piece-by-piece, nothing seemed to fit together. It was as if I lived in a big sprawling mansion with plenty of rooms, all of which were separated by long, dark hallways, and I kept getting lost on my way from one room to the next. Like a stately, colonial house, my life looked fine on the outside; on the inside, however, my life was cordoned off, with each room disconnected from the others. This lifestyle—this separating, packaging, and hiding—was fine, I suppose, when life was moving along smoothly, but as soon as there was a bump in the road or something was amiss in one of the rooms—a casserole burning in the oven, broken shingles on the roof, a broken computer, a mountain of toys in the playroom—well, forget about it. There was no way I'd be able to make it from one room to the next, down those long, dark hallways. Emotions escalated far sooner than necessary, my moods more volatile. Tears were an almost daily occurrence, and I grew impatient with just about everyone and everything. But even more than the emotions, the moods, the tears, and the impatience was this constant sense of emptiness and disorientation. I felt like I had been dropped onto some faraway island where everyone knew the language, the customs, and the culture while I was fumbling with an out-of-date translation guide.

I felt lost and out of place.

And as I walked those metaphorical hallways, I kept hearing that voice—sometimes meek and a little desperate, other times raucous and eager—asking, *Isn't there something more? Isn't there a way to break down these walls and bring it all together?*

And the answer came, slowly and gently, but unmistakably.

Grace. Wonder. Miracles.

These beautiful mysteries break down the walls of our boxy, brick colonials and build bright, airy lofts with tall windows that let in the sunlight, casting reverberations of the sacred and an undercurrent of spirituality. Connecting, joining, reuniting.

Grace. Wonder. Miracles. They gently lift the lids on all the boxes we carry, gradually release the torn and tattered pieces, and tie the frayed edges together with a silken thread.

Grace. Wonder. Miracles.

We are hungry, starving, almost *ravenous* for a sacred connection that will tie together the frayed edges and ragged fragments of our lives, to feel some kind of reassurance that if we open up the boxes, we won't end up in a heap of lost brokenness. We are desperate to know that there is something more than the madness and chaos of our daily lives—that there is something more than credit card bills and medical problems and strained relationships, but we're also terrified about what might happen if there is not.

So we separate. We package. We hide.

But like some massive chicken-or-the-egg conundrum, we can't feel that *something more*, we can't experience sacred connection, and we can't really know God if we don't break open the boxes first.

I suppose it is necessary here to explain my use of the word "God." Was there ever a word as dangerously divisive, or as compassionately empowering, as that tiny three-letter word? Few words have the power to conjure up such powerful emotions, whether it's fear, apprehension, devotion, or serenity as the word *God*. But when you get down to it, that's all it really is—a word. It's a linguistic limitation used to describe a mysterious and unknowable cosmic energy, a phonetic placeholder for our own personal mental images, whether they be of spiritual networks or powerful creators or patient parents or comforting mentors.

God is a word that means different things to different people. I use the word *God* to describe the vast, hidden web of interconnectedness between all living and nonliving things in the universe. God has always been a driving force in my life, even when I didn't have a firm grasp on my specific beliefs or know whether I even believed in God. To me, God is affection, patience, and mercy; God is also bitterness, jealousy, and regret. God is what links the dusty particles of my body to the dusty particles of yours. God is the shooting star, the nitrogen that fertilizes the plants during a spring thunderstorm, and the seashore erosion caused by crashing waves.

God—to me—is in everything and everyone, God is everything and everyone, and God connects everything and everyone. How could one three-letter word possibly be expected to adequately convey all of that?

The truth is, it can't. Regardless of how you think of God or the definitions and characteristics you identify with God, the word remains a linguistic representation of something that will always remain intangible and unknowable for us. And that is difficult for us to understand and accept. We are limited by our semantic expressions and connotations. But the force of that concept, the sacred connection that it creates, is limitless.

In this book, I use the word *God* as the driving force behind grace, wonder, and everyday miracles. God is synonymous with Divine Source, Loving Unifier, and Sacred Connector.

God is the Box-Opener and Thread-Weaver.

Some people believe in a God who is reserved for religion, for the rule-followers and unquestioning believers. But this is not the God I believe in. Rather, for me, God is grace and wonder and miracles. In fact, sometimes I wonder why we take something so personal and indescribable and feel like we need to muck it up with rules and dogma. But God (at least by my definition) isn't reserved for the members of this religion or that religion, or even just for the believers.

And isn't that the really great thing about God, or whatever word you use when you talk about that indescribable force? That it will always be (can only be!) something so uniquely personal that it is almost beyond language?

God, to me, lives in and around each of us. The sacred isn't reserved for churches with tall steeples and stained glass windows; it's found in dark bars and at our kitchen tables and in shopping mall parking lots. God's voice isn't spoken only to and through priests, rabbis, and shamans; it's heard in the music we hum in the car, in a dog-eared book, in our children's voices, in a raspy voice whispering somewhere inside, *Open the boxes and I'll tie you together with grace, with wonder, with miracles.*

And we want to shout back in response, "Yes, I knew it all along!"

I first found grace as a young girl. Standing in an old church, clutching my hymnal, I was fully prepared to mouth along with the choir's song to meet the requisite level of "participation." But as soon as I heard the tune, sung soft and low, I couldn't help but join in.

Amazing Grace, how sweet the sound, that saved a wretch like me.

6

Something about the words, the melody, and this grace thing that we were singing about compelled me to sing. In fact, I couldn't *not* sing.

I had heard about God a million times—in church, from my parents, at school, from friends—but at this young age, I was still a little uncertain about who or what God was. I wasn't really even sure if I believed in God at that point. All I knew was that I *should* believe in God. Whatever God was.

But grace? No one ever told me who or what grace was, let alone whether it was something holy. Yet something about that word, about the feelings it created and the actions it embodied, told me that grace was a divine force to be reckoned with, that grace could change lives, and that grace was really the thing that mattered.

Turns out, as I have seen over and over again since I first sang that song as a child, grace is really just God made known. If God is energy, grace is the light switch. If God is a noun, grace is a verb. If God is, grace does. As the theologian Karl Barth once said, "Grace must find expression in life, otherwise it is not grace."[2]

Grace is often used but seldom understood and even more difficult to explain (though writers, preachers, and poets have been trying to do so for years). Grace, for me, isn't so much a definable word, as it is something that must be felt. Like the colloquial expression first made famous by Supreme Court Justice Potter Stewart in *Jacobellis v. Ohio*, "I know it when I see it."[3]

With grace's parameters as a manifestation of the Divine, acting as a bridge between the sacred and the secular, it becomes far easier to see, feel, touch, and know God. Grace is God's voice heard through a stranger's kind words, a dear friend's voice, or a song on the radio. Grace is God's face seen in a young child's smile, a cascading waterfall, or memories of a beloved grandmother. Grace is God's

---

[2] Helmut Gollwitzer, *An Introduction to Protestant Theology* (Louisville: Westminster Press, 1982), 174.
[3] *Jacobellis v. Ohio*, 378 U.S. 184 (1964).

hand felt through a soft embrace, by practicing yoga, or when swimming underwater.

While grace's definition may be hard to explain, its power is not. As Anne Lamott wrote, "I do not at all understand the mystery of grace—only that it meets us where we are, but does not leave us where it found us."[4] Grace saves, grace teaches, grace transforms.

Bestselling author and minister Max Lucado wrote, "Grace is God walking into your world with a sparkle in his eye and an offer that's hard to resist . . . Grace is simply another word for God's tumbling, rumbling reservoir of strength and protection. It comes at us not occasionally or miserly but constantly and aggressively. Wave upon wave."[5]

If grace is a manifestation of the Divine, then wonder is the heart-stopping, incomprehensible reaction to that manifestation. There are some things that are just so fantastically *good*, so pure and lovely, so breathtakingly beautiful, that we are nearly brought to our knees with astonishment and gratitude. Sleeping babies. Double rainbows. Tiny huts over Tahitian blue waters. Fresh snow on pine trees. Frozen peanut- butter cups. Military homecomings. Hot sand between toes. Laughing until you cry. There are no words, only a sense of grateful wonder and contented awe.

And there are some things that are just so dreadfully painful, so senseless and absurd, so cruel and harsh, that we are nearly brought to our knees with desperation and incredulity. Suicide bombings. Pediatric cancer. F5 tornadoes. Friends that move away. Pink slips. War. There are no words, only a sense of confused wonder and distressed awe.

Wonder is childlike curiosity, deep reverence and amazement, and a constant questioning all wrapped into one. Anne Lamott refers to wonder as the third great prayer:

––––––––––––––––

[4] Anne Lamott, *Traveling Mercies: Some Thoughts on Faith,* (New York: Anchor Books, 1999), 143.
[5] Max Lucado, *Grace: More Than We Deserve, Greater Than We Imagine,* (Nashville: Thomas Nelson, 2012), 74, 94.

The third great prayer, Wow, is often uttered with a gasp, a sharp intake of breath, when we can't think of another way to capture the sight of shocking beauty or destruction, of a sudden unbidden insight or an unexpected flash of grace. "Wow" means we are not dulled to wonder.[6]

She goes on to say, "What can we say beyond Wow, in the presence of glorious art, in music so magnificent that it can't have originated solely on this side of things? Wonder takes our breath away, and makes room for new breath."[7]

Not only does wonder take our breath away, but it holds us captive for a few moments to the magic and mystery. It holds open a space between the question and any possible answer, whispering *let's just rest here a bit.* Wonder tingles, tantalizes, stills, and calms. It holds our amazement and our anger, our reverence and frustration.

Grace opens the boxes, while wonder holds them open for as a long as it takes for the contents to tumble out. Wonder gently places all those muddled pieces—the heartbreak and the addictions, the forgiveness and the hope, the questions and the fears, the love and the mercy, the shame and the humility—gently next to each other, wiping them clean and tending to them with a gentle hand, so they are prepped for the needle and thread.

So that *we* are ready for the needle and thread. So that we can see the miracles—not just the big miracles like cures for cancer and men on the moon, but *everyday* miracles. Coffee with a good friend. A handwritten letter of gratitude. Food on the table. Airplanes. A job offer. The Internet.

Albert Einstein said, "There are only two ways to live your life. One is as though nothing is a miracle; the other is as though everything is a miracle."

---

[6] Anne Lamott, *Help Thanks Wow: The Three Essential Prayers,* (New York: Riverhead Books, 2012), 71.
[7] Lamott, *Help Thanks Wow,* 81.

Some people choose to live as though there is an explanation for everything, believing that most questions can be answered by determining the value of the missing variable in the equation, even if the variable is just luck and coincidence. For some people, nothing is a miracle; everything is explainable.

Me, I choose the other way. The everything-is-a-miracle way. Despite the fact that I am a logical, pragmatic, and somewhat reasonable person, there is *always* a touch of miracle to everything. Waking up in the morning. Miracle. The changing seasons. Miracle. Friendship and marriage and learning to read. All miracles. Of course, there are Point-A-to-Point-B rational reasons that friendships continue and marriages thrive and children learn to read that probably have a lot to do with our brain chemistry and nerve impulses and evolution and hard work. And yet there is a hint of the inexplicable and a trace of oh-so-good-ness in it that it has to be a miracle. It is just *too good* to solely attribute to dumb luck or random chance or scientific rationality. It has to be a miracle because were it not, it just wouldn't feel quite so good.

Lemony Snicket (*aka* Daniel Handler) wrote in *The Lump of Coal*, "Miracles are like pimples because once you start looking for them, you find more than you ever dreamed you'd see."[8] So many more!

Miracles every day. And everyday miracles.

Grace. Wonder. Miracles. With them, the needle moves over, under, and through all those frayed edges, all those tattered scraps and disjointed fragments. It is just that simple . . . and just that difficult. The stories you are about to read prove it.

Earlier, I talked about how I felt lost and disoriented for much of my life. I felt a bit disconnected and confused with lots of big, nagging questions about purpose, identity, and my place in all of this. I looked for answers in a lot of places and in a lot of ways, but ultimately it all led back to the same thing; there was one common

---

[8] Lemony Snicket, *The Lump of Coal*, (New York: HarperCollins Children's Books, 2008).

denominator connecting it all: spirituality. As soon as I stopped separating spirituality from everything else and came to terms with the idea that spirituality is inextricably a part of *everything*, the lens turned ever so slightly and things started to come into focus.

I don't know if I can go so far as to say that I was "found," but I do know that I no longer felt quite so lost, disoriented, or disconnected. Instead of wandering the long, dark hallways from room to room looking for answers and seeking *something*, a string of tiny lights came into focus, illuminating a path, and connecting every room in the house.

There are many ways that we can experience the thread of spirituality in our lives. Some people find it through yoga or meditation, while others find it through long walks, gardening, or volunteering. Me, I find the ropes of spirituality and strings of flickering lights in grace, wonder, and everyday miracles. As you will see in the stories and words that line the pages of this book, these are not big light-bulb moments. They aren't sudden epiphanies or extraordinary once-in-a-lifetime events. They are the tiny moments, the gradual realizations, the slow awakenings, and the seemingly ordinary goings-on that make up our days and our lives. They are so tiny and so ordinary, in fact, that they are at risk of being overlooked or taken for granted. Like caterpillars or rose petals or rainbows in muddy puddles. But when we put on our new lenses—when we look *for* them and look *at* them, when we honor these small moments with big meaning—we bring things into focus. We find the illuminated string of lights that is spirituality. We tie it all together.

Shauna Niequist wrote, "The world is alive, blinking and clicking, winking at us slyly, inviting us to get up and dance to the music that's been playing since the beginning of time, if you bend all the way down and put your ear to the ground to listen to it."[9]

Let's listen. Let's dance. Let's celebrate.

---

[9] Shauna Niequist, *Cold Tangerines,* (Grand Rapids: Zondervan, 2007), 11.

Let's open boxes and look closely at what lies inside, because laced within all the mess and grit are glittery sprinkles of God. Amidst all the madness and chaos is a gossamer thread of sacred connection.

Let's open boxes and tie threads. Let's weave and stitch. Let's live fully and connect deeply.

Grace

"You can have the other words—chance, luck, coincidence, serendipity. I'll take grace. I don't know what it is exactly, but I'll take it."

—Mary Oliver

Divine Kindness in an Old Navy Parking Lot

"Beginning today, treat everyone you meet as if
they were going to be dead by midnight. Extend
to them all the care, kindness and understanding
you can muster, and do it with no thought of any
reward. Your life will never be the same again."
—Og Mandino

One doesn't expect to experience divine intervention in an Old Navy parking lot. One expects to leave Old Navy with a trendy, ill-fitting pair of pants or too many V-neck sweaters. But coming face to face with God in an Old Navy parking lot? Never. God saves himself for churches and synagogues and dark basements where AA meetings are held on metal folding chairs. God does not show up at Old Navy.

At least, that's what I thought, too, until that white teddy bear showed up.

Sitting front and center inside the doors of Old Navy, the teddy bear proudly flaunted its blue scarf and beckoned to be cuddled. It was at least as big as my two-year-old son so, naturally, he just *had* to have it.

"Honey, we aren't getting a teddy bear today," I feebly replied to his pleas. "We are just here to get you new mittens."

But, like most kids his age, my son was relentless, and I was tired. I was so very tired. Not just bone-tired, but soul-tired. It was the fall of 2008 and, like just about every other American, our family was feeling the crushing weight of financial stress and job insecurities. I had grown weary from the constant strain of it all.

I was tired, I was weary, and I was broken. Spirit-broken and heart-broken. Having just suffered my third miscarriage in six months, I was angry at just about everyone and everything—angry at the bad luck, angry at the horrible circumstances, angry at my body, angry at God, and angry at whatever or whoever was responsible for this wretchedness.

I was tired, I was broken, and I was weak.

So I caved.

I let him carry that big white bear throughout the store with the intention of returning it when we were done with our shopping trip. After I had retrieved the requisite mittens and hat, I confidently strode up to the checkout aisle, patting myself on the back for our quick tantrum-free shopping excursion. I set the mittens and hat on the counter and gently pried the bear from my son's tiny hands so that I could give it to the clerk, politely telling her we had changed our mind about the bear. But when I picked it up, its round bottom was now a dingy black, evidence of the dirt and grime from the floor.

I let out an audible groan and meekly asked the clerk how much the bear cost, knowing that because we had ruined it, we would now be buying it.

"Twenty dollars," the young woman responded.

I let out a louder groan. *Dammit!* I did not want to spend twenty dollars. I did not want my son to think that he could get whatever he wanted. And I did not want this beastly teddy bear taking up more space in our already cramped home.

"Okay," I sighed. "I guess we'll be buying that as well."

As I was pulling out my wallet and trying to keep my grabby-hands son from making any more unintended purchases, I heard a voice nearby chide, "That's what you get."

I looked around and quickly realized that the acerbic voice was coming from the shriveled woman behind me. And the voice wasn't stopping. She continued to tell me how I should have known better, how I should have done better, and how I should have been better. Her litany of callous advice went on and on.

Rage—pure, unadulterated rage—boiled up inside me. The fighter in me instantly came to life. I wanted to scream. I wanted to slap her. And I also wanted to curl up in a ball and sob.

I took a breath, summoned every ounce of strength I could find, and turned to this prune of a woman.

"Are you a mother?" I asked.

"Yes, of course I am."

"Perhaps then you might understand just how hard it is," I squeaked in a mouse-like voice.

"I would never have let my kids drag a teddy bear around the store," she retorted. "You need to set limits."

As she threw her judgments and criticism at me, all I could think was, *What have I done to deserve such harsh criticism? What have I done to deserve being berated by a stranger when I was merely trying to buy a pair of mittens?*

What have I done to deserve any of this—the criticism, the miscarriages, the infertility problems, the financial setbacks, the loneliness, the cruelty of strangers?

Why does the universe seem to be so against me? Why, in God's name, is everything so damn hard? And where is this supposed God to help me through this crap?

Enough, I thought. *Enough. I give up.*

I had no fight left in me.

"Thank you," I responded, for the first time surrendering myself to a higher power and something bigger than my own fragile emotions. "I appreciate your advice."

I turned back to the clerk and handed her my credit card. After signing the receipt, I grabbed my purchases, took my son's hand as he clutched the beastly teddy bear, and marched out of the store—which, because I was dealing with an uncoordinated toddler and a cumbersome three-foot-tall teddy bear, was much slower and less dramatic than I would have liked.

More tired, more broken, and weaker than ever, I tried to hustle my son to the car so I could have an emotional breakdown in private, but we weren't more than a few steps out of the store when a red sedan pulled up to the curb. The driver, a round-faced man who looked to be in his early forties, leaned across the seat.

"Excuse me," the man said as I braced myself for another confrontation. "I just wanted to tell you that I saw what happened in the store. I was humbled and amazed. You handled that situation beautifully and I am inspired. *You* have inspired me. I will carry that with me the rest of the day as I try to be a better person. Thank you."

And just like that, the red sedan drove off. I stood there on the curb for a few moments, stunned and marveling at the profound impact this odd group of strangers had all had on each other. Afterward, I sat in the car for what felt like hours, but was probably just a few minutes. While my son clutched his new, (mostly) white teddy bear, a few tears rolled down my cheeks. When I looked at him in the rearview mirror, I smiled, knowing that eventually everything would be all right. That everything was *already* all right.

I needn't have wondered about the universe's hostility or humanity's cruelty. Everything I had doubted was clearer now than ever before, because on that cool, fall day, God had shown up in an Old Navy parking lot dressed as a round-faced, forty-year-old man driving a red sedan. God showed up as kindness and grace.

Human kindness is a core value of many of the world's religions. Christianity teaches of the importance of kindness through compassion and mercy; Hinduism teaches that "the sum of duty [is to] do not to others what would cause pain if done to you." Sikhism imparts that everyone should be treated with kindness, as they are not strangers. Unitarian Universalists promote respect for the "interdependent web of all existence of which we are a part." Humanists rely on the "Golden Rule." Confucius taught that loving kindness sums up the basis of all good conduct. Perhaps the Dalai Lama said it best, though: "My religion is very simple. My religion is kindness."

But all of these teachings can only go so far if the *idea* of kindness is not acted upon. If kindness only consists of kind thoughts, it has achieved only half its purpose. Kindness must be shared, in act and deed, to achieve its full and complete divine purpose.

It can be overwhelming to realize that our actions have the ability to affect someone else and the greater whole. There is an amazing empowerment, but also a great vulnerability, that comes with the realization that everything we do matters, that every moment is a chance to create a miracle. Kindness as God in action requires effort and proactivity, both of which can be hard—*very* hard—at times.

A few months ago, I went through a restaurant's drive-thru and the woman who took my money had the most beautiful blue eye shadow. It was a stunning shade of peacock blue, applied with an expert hand. As I waited for my food, I considered telling her just how much I liked her eye shadow, but I worried that I might make her feel uncomfortable. Or that she might think of me as a crazy lady in the minivan commenting on blue eye shadow at eleven in the morning. So, ultimately, I said nothing. I took my food, thanked her, and drove off.

But what difference might I have made if I had paid her an unexpected compliment? If I had *acted in kindness* instead of just thinking kind thoughts?

Maybe she was a mom, with little time to take care of herself, and didn't always feel very attractive. Maybe she had quarreled with her spouse that morning and could have used a kind word. Maybe the eye shadow was a fancy splurge that she second-guessed and berated herself for buying. Maybe the compliment would have brightened her day just enough to cause her to be more patient with her co-workers and customers. Or maybe she would have thought of me as the crazy lady in the minivan. Who knows?

Regardless, I held the power to *share* kindness, to spread warmth, to act with grace, and I didn't do anything because I was embarrassed and shy and worried about what someone might think of me.

What a shame.

Sometimes it really takes just the smallest act of kindness to make a world of difference. It might be as simple as looking a homeless man in the eye and touching his hand when we drop a few dollars into his basket. It might mean telling a haggard-looking mom that she's doing a good—no, *great*—job. It might be as simple as picking up the tab for a guy in army fatigues sitting in the restaurant booth behind us. It might be as simple as smiling at every person we see throughout the day.

Every encounter with a fellow human being is a chance to act in grace and an opportunity to be God's instrument. It's a chance to change someone's life.

In any situation, there is a chance to play a role in the human story. We can be the critical woman in Old Navy doling out judgments and criticism. We can be my inner warrior, lashing out and striking back with even more anger and hostility. We can be the resigned peacekeeper who calms the situation and wards off further escalation. Or we can be the kind stranger who changes lives, improves someone else's day, and makes things just a little bit better. We can be a transmitter of compassion and benevolence. We can be a manifestation of the Divine. We can be God in action.

Ask yourself: *Who do I want to be? Who am I going to be? And how will I act in accordance with that?*

As Mother Theresa said, "We can do no great things, only small things with great love."

We can do small things with great kindness.

We can open boxes with grace.

Superheroes and Bunkmates

"Sometimes being a brother is even better than being a superhero."
—Marc Brown

Each summer, our suburban town hosts concerts in the park on Friday nights. Since we live just a few blocks from the park where the concerts are held, my husband and I try to take our kids as often as possible. But with two young, rambunctious boys, it's sometimes difficult to enjoy the concert. The boys usually find a few of their friends and spend the hour or so that we are there running around, dancing, and generally being silly.

On one occasion, we had met a few friends and were chatting along the edge of the crowd during the show. The boys raced about, and I watched them out of the corner of my eye as they blended into the crowd of children running, dancing, and playing. Jackson was old enough to venture off on his own a little, but Teddy was young enough to require constant supervision. So I cocked my head half toward our friends as they talked about the weather, the band, and weekend plans. But I couldn't really listen. I was distracted, too captivated by my boys.

As they cavorted about with the other kids, caught up in a rowdy game of tag, Teddy was struggling to keep up with the older kids. He was always a step or two behind, yet he persevered by intently studying and following their every move.

The band switched songs and played louder. More children began to gather toward the front of the stage, and the boys continued their game of running and chasing with some other kids.

Suddenly, Teddy found himself lost in the throngs of children. He scanned the crowd, first with annoyance and then with increasing panic. Soon he was visibly paralyzed with fear, becoming swallowed by a mob of children. I saw him quickly call out once, twice, then three times—not for me or his dad, but for his older brother Jackson. His head searched the crowd, quickly turning left, then right, then left again.

Just as I was about to swoop in to rescue him and ward off any potential tears, Jackson emerged. I watched, awestruck, as he held out his hand to his younger brother and guided him out of the fray. I watched, fascinated, as he placed his hand on the back of Teddy's neck. I felt calm as he led him out of the frenzied maze of dancing children.

Siblings are often our first experience with grace. They teach us how to communicate, interact, share, compromise, and develop our own voice. Siblings can be a partner in crime, a confidant, and a protector. Siblings give us roots by grounding us to home and family and tradition, and wings by providing a soft place to land.

Siblings also drive us absolutely mad sometimes.

As a child, I shared a bedroom with my sister, Carrie. Like most siblings, we had a love-hate relationship for much of our childhood. We fought fiercely. We shared resignedly. And we loved unconditionally.

Carrie and I taped lines down the center of the room and used black permanent marker to indicate "mine" and "yours." We slammed doors and locked each other out. And we clashed, physically sometimes, until blood was drawn. We also confided in each other, whispering late into the night under the soft glow of the moon. And we defended each other, allying ourselves against our parents, peers, or the world in general.

My years with Carrie in that one tiny room was a sort of heaven and hell all wrapped into one. With only a year and a half separating us in age, we shared many of the same experiences and the same friends throughout our youth. My highs were her highs; her lows were my lows. I desperately wanted independence, but I thrived with the companionship and solidarity and love-until-it-hurts-ness.

We were like two sides of the same coin, different but always together. So much so that when I left for college and slept apart from Carrie for the first time in seventeen years, I felt like a limb had been severed. After all, we are sisters. And that, I think, explains it all.

Similarly, when my brother moved away a few years ago after living nearby for the previous three, the pain was so shocking and fierce that I was certain my heart had broken into a million little pieces that were rushing out of my body as tears.

Countless books have been written about siblings, and I'm sure billions of dollars are spent each year to pay psychologists and therapists who help us muddle our way through "sibling issues," but most of the books and rhetoric miss out on one subtle but essential component of the sibling relationship: siblings share a tiny piece of our soul as much as they share a few strands of DNA. A relationship so wrought with genetic, emotional, and experiential connections, along with an inherent *spiritual* connection, is not always an easy one to explain or navigate. It is fraught with disagreements and quarrels and annoyances, those scrapes and bruises and scars that come from bumping elbows so closely with another human being.

And yet . . .

There is a common spiritual DNA, a double helix twisted with mercy, desperation, and understanding. There is grace. Not just in the laughter and in the seeing eye to eye, but also in the moments when we lead a brother out of a frenzied fray, when the lines drawn down the center of a shared bedroom are removed, when a locked door is opened, and when the separation hurts us more than the challenges that come with living together.

I wasn't necessarily thinking all of these things that night in the park as I watched my boys separate, struggle, and find each other again. I'm not sure I was thinking anything. Perhaps the flood of emotions and the wave of grace that washed over me obliterated any coherent thoughts. But as I walked home later that night, pushing Teddy in the stroller while my husband carried Jackson on his shoulders, I looked at my boys and smiled. I thanked God and the universe and my husband for assembling together our motley group of mischief. I prayed that I'd never forget the gratitude and awe and grace that enveloped me that night as I am wont to do when I get caught up in the busyness of carpools, homework, baseball practice, and work deadlines, when I'm bulldozed by fights over Legos, and when my sole purpose in life seems to be playing referee to he-said-he-said debates. And I prayed that they would never forget those sibling things as well, which we so often do as we drift apart geographically and spiritually and emotionally. I prayed that years from now, when the worlds of these brothers are wider and more complicated than they could ever imagine, they would remember that they were each other's first friend, ally, leader, and protector. That when they have jobs, families, and kids of their own, they would continue to call out to each other amidst the chaos of their daily lives. That when their problems consist not of skinned knees and broken toys, but of financial struggles, career setbacks, and relationship challenges, they would continue to hold out a hand to each other. That when they are confused and hurt and frustrated and lost, they would be the first one to guide the other to safety.

I prayed that they would always—*always*—be more than siblings, that they would be brothers guided by and grounded in grace.

Where Are the Backrubs?

*"Knowledge of the self is the mother of all knowledge.
So it is incumbent on me to know myself, to know it
completely, to know its minutiae, its characteristics, its
subtleties, and its very atoms."*
—Khalil Gibran

When I first met my husband, all fresh-faced and confused, I told him a teensy-tiny little white lie.

I told him I wanted to be a massage therapist.

Given that I was in law school at the time, this statement should have raised a few eyebrows and begged a few questions.

Instead, like most twenty-four-year-old men, he simply responded with, "Wow. That's cool. Maybe I could get a backrub some day?"

Fifteen years later, he's still waiting. At last, in writing this, I think I might concede that perhaps massage therapy was not my divine calling.

But, oh how I wanted it to be my calling. How I *wanted* to make a living helping other people feel better physically and mentally. How I wanted to embody the laidback, peaceful zen that I imagined massage therapists would personify. How I wanted to escape the mental rigor of the legal field and the emotional turmoil brewing inside my head and heart. Wouldn't a calm career—one that involved a constant stream of tranquil meditation music and soft candlelight—be the perfect way to do that? And, most importantly, wouldn't a hip and sexy job like massage therapy be the perfect way to impress this new beau of mine?

As it is for many young people—women, especially—my teens and twenties were a season of life filled with a significant amount of doubt, betrayal, and fear. I was tired of feeling boring and predictable. I was tired of feeling demure and uptight. I was tired of the person I had been for the previous twenty-something years, so I pretended to be something and someone I was not: fun, sexy, laidback, and hip. This is what I wanted to be, this is what I pretended to be. I wanted to be someone I wasn't so I said I would become something I couldn't be. I wanted to impress, I wanted to change. Like a snake that can no longer hold the painful stretch of its old skin, I wanted to shed it and move onto something new.

Turns out, I was pretty good at pretending. I was an expert at fooling myself so it never really felt like I was being inauthentic. Growing up in a small, fairly conservative town in central Wisconsin, I spent most of my life thinking I held certain political, religious, and social beliefs. I fit into the role created for me, whether by teachers, friends, peers, family, society, and the one I created for myself.

I got so good at pretending, meeting expectations, and fulfilling a role that eventually I didn't really know the version of *me* I wanted to be, let alone the *me* I really was.

So there we were, my husband and I, flirting and falling in love, with me walking onto the stage in a different costume every other scene. Honestly, it's a wonder he was even able to keep up with the cast of characters!

Several years later, after much introspection and long conversations with God—through a lot of growing pains, and with a heaping dose of forgiveness and healing—I think I am finally coming into my own skin, the skin that was underneath all the costumes.

And who is that person, exactly?

Well, honestly, I'm not always sure, and it's certainly not easily defined in soundbites or labels. What I am sure of, however, is that I no longer want to persuade myself and others that I am someone other than who I am, even if that someone is just a woman meandering her way through life in the most authentic way possible.

And as I look back, I wish that I had learned the art of authenticity—and flexibility—a little sooner, instead of making firm plans and spouting absolutes. Like Shauna Niequist said in *Cold Tangerines*,[10] I wish I had written in pencil. I wish I had said, "I don't know" and "maybe" more, and asked "what about . . .?" and "what if I . . . ?" more. I wish I had been less certain and more open to possibility. I wish I had been less rigid and more fluid. I wish I had been more comfortable with and in the questions, and less eager to rush to conclusions and judgments. I wish I had spent less time pretending and more time being real and authentic, more *me*.

Faith has always been a big question mark for me, a place where I did a lot of pretending and role-filling and believing by osmosis. I went to church on Easter and Christmas and a few dozen Sundays in between. I said the Lord's Prayer and the Nicene Creed. I moved my hands to make the sign of the cross. But an authentic faith and a personal spirituality eluded me. I believed what I was told to believe, followed the rules and rituals I was told to follow, and left matters of authentic faith to those more enlightened than me. An authentic faith was something for aging hippies and New Age yoga instructors; it was not something for a shy girl from a rural Wisconsin town who was raised to genuflect before sliding into a church pew and to avoid meat on Fridays during Lent. An authentic faith was something for the "brave ones" or those who simply had nothing to lose. I, on the other hand, had a whole family I would disappoint and a whole culture I would lose if I were to embrace an authentic faith that ventured

---

[10] Niequist, *Cold Tangerines*, 203.

away from my inherited faith. In other words, an authentic faith was a luxury I couldn't afford.

But sometimes we just don't have a choice in the matter and our truth comes looking for us. I know this is true because I found my truth when I fell into the "belief gap" during my Spiritual Breakdown, and soon realized I couldn't afford to live without feeding an authentic faith.

Of course, my Spiritual Breakdown had to come on a holiday. (Don't the really big things—the life-changing moments, the callings, and the a-ha moments—always happen at the most inconvenient times?) There I sat that Christmas Eve afternoon, on a wooden pew like so many other wooden pews I had sat on in my life. The church was new to me; it was the closest church to my in-laws' house that held a Christmas Eve mass, yet it was like so many other churches. Stained glass and pointed ceilings, exposed wood beams and long aisles. I sat on that wooden pew, smoothed out my skirt, and glanced at my watch.

The congregation began to sing its opening hymn, probably "Silent Night" or "Oh, Come, All Ye Faithful," and I sang along, quietly. I shifted in my seat, uncomfortably warm in my winter coat, but too confined to move my arms out of my sleeves. This was the Christmas Eve mass after all.

The opening hymn concluded. We sat. The priest greeted us. Prayers were read. I glanced at my watch again.

Like most Christmas Eve masses, this was a family service. Children were everywhere, the girls dressed in red velvet dresses with black bows that tied in the back, the boys in crisp white shirts with brand-new sweater vests purchased just for this occasion. The congregation's children had rehearsed a short play depicting the Christmas story.

Mary, played by a young girl about eleven or twelve years old, walked across the front of the church and, well, you know the rest. She and her tween Joseph searched and searched for an inn. No luck.

As I sat there in that wooden pew like so many other wooden pews, hearing a story I had heard so many other times, I realized I was having what I've come to know as a Spiritual Breakdown. In a flash of intense emotion and rational clarity, I realized that everything I had believed, or that I had been told to believe, just didn't ring true for me. The children continued with their presentation of Jesus' birth and all I could think was: *What if? What about? What then?*

I tried to let my doubts and questions simmer, hoping they would pass. But like Mary and Joseph's attempt to find an inn, I had no luck, and my uncertainties only grew stronger. Decades of inherited and duplicated beliefs began to fall away one by one, quickly and smoothly, until I was left with a tiny nugget that might have looked a little bit like authenticity, but I was too afraid to look.

The service droned on. I squirmed as my mind wandered. *Is my new baby boy, just two months old, all right at home with my in-laws? Is he crying or sleeping? How much longer will this service go on? Will I ever get any sleep? How annoyed will the rest of the family be that we were late to the party so I could attend Christmas Eve mass?*

Amidst all of my mind's practical wanderings lay the crushing, heavy weight of my newfound theological catharsis. Traditional Christmas hymns occasionally interrupted my anxious reveries, but the songs that had once moved and lifted me, lightening my mood and calming my soul, now disturbed me. The lyrics were triggers for the doubts, like salt to a fresh wound desperately trying to heal.

Finally, the service ended and my husband and I fled. In fact, we may have even made the typical "Catholic exit," leaving after communion but before the end of the service. As we walked out the doors to the soft hum of the mass's final song, the snow was gently beginning to fall, setting the stage for a proverbial Christmas scene, one that I immediately shattered when I turned to my husband and blurted out all of my doubts, anger, and frustration at the seeming absurdity of religion.

"Quiet," he whispered wryly. "We're still in the parking lot. We could be struck down by lightning if you say things like that here."

I chuckled, both amused and annoyed at his attempt at humor. I had long grown accustomed to Matt's use of comedy to diffuse a stressful situation, but I was annoyed that he hadn't taken my doubts and beliefs seriously. Looking back, he probably thought these doubts and frustrations were just another passing whim, another example of my emotional personality and flair for dramatics, another one of those flighty cast members that fluttered across the stage of my being from time to time. And rightfully so, for just a few years earlier when we met, I had been regularly attending services most weekends, wore a cross pendant, and frequently listened to gospel music while studying for law school finals.

The enormity of my Spiritual Breakdown was profoundly unsettling to me. I was raised in a devoutly Catholic family, going to church every Sunday without fail, and I had always been a faithful Christian. Sure, my church attendance ebbed at various times in my life, and I was by no means a religious zealot. I was a young woman who like so many others had inherited a faith and carried on that faith. I wasn't flashy or fanatical in my faith. I didn't proselytize. I followed some religious prescriptions—regular church attendance, confession, alms giving, and certain dietary restrictions, for instance. Other religious rules I found to be impractical and paid them little heed—prohibitions on premarital sex, alcohol, stem cell research, and contraceptives, to name a few. But through it all, I was faithful. I was religious. I was Christian.

Until the Spiritual Breakdown, of course.

We returned to my in-laws' house for a secular Christmas Eve celebration. Family members cooed over our new baby, the first in the next generation. We exchanged gifts; a personally engraved baseball bat for my infant son was the highlight gift of the year. We ate. We drank. I tried to enjoy the festivities, but with the extreme sleep deprivation I was experiencing, fun was difficult.

I remember little of the rest of that Christmas holiday, except for the three-hour drive from Chicago to Wisconsin the next morning, where we were to celebrate the holiday with my parents, grandparents, siblings, and extended family. During that drive, our sweet newborn dozed peacefully. And, as he slept, the Spiritual Breakdown continued. I sobbed, my head in my hands and tears quietly streaming down my face, until, like a newborn baby, I was spent and tearless.

The crushing weight of emotions that accompany first-time motherhood forced me to succumb to the enormity of the emptiness I had been feeling. Not only did hormones, sleep deprivation, and anxiety leave me feeling hollow and angry much of the time, but I no longer had a faith to rely on. I felt betrayed by everyone. Betrayed by my son because he didn't sleep more. Betrayed by my family for the endless unsolicited advice. Betrayed by my body for yielding to the rigors of childbirth. Betrayed by my husband for not reading my mind. Betrayed by whatever faith I had once had for abandoning me when I felt most vulnerable. Betrayed by religion, betrayed by God, and most of all, betrayed by myself for being consumed by irrational, illogical, unhappy thoughts.

Matt and I survived the remainder of the Christmas season with little discussion about my Spiritual Breakdown, but my doubts and fears lingered. The more I considered questions regarding faith—or whatever had once resembled a faith—the more I realized I had no idea what I believed anymore. The Spiritual Breakdown had pushed me over the edge of a cliff and I had fallen into "the Belief Gap," as historian and author Diana Butler Bass calls it in her book *Christianity After Religion: The End of Church and the Birth of a New Spiritual Awakening*—a scary place for anyone to be, let alone someone as vulnerable and shaken as I was.

But there is something interesting about falling into the Belief Gap, whether it has to do with faith, career, family, eating habits, or self-image, and that is this: once you've fallen into the deep gorge, having stripped away all the branches and smoothed out all the foothills that had always brought a sense of security and reassurance, you can finally see all the way to the bottom. And down there rests a tiny little gem of authenticity that twinkles like the stars and shines a light as bright as the sun.

The Spiritual Breakdown eventually led to the Spiritual Awakening, with an inherent truth that burrowed to my very core and into the very essence of my soul. In some respects, the Spiritual Breakdown was like a sudden and unexpected bolt of lightning, scorching everything I had once known. In other respects, the Spiritual Breakdown was more of a bubbling volcano, spilling hot lava that peeled away the layers of my inherited faith. Either way, the end result was the same: this Spiritual Breakdown cleared a path for an authentic faith lined with grace, honesty, and personal truth, and would lead me straight into God's web.

Years later, I still have days when the challenges associated with living out an authentic faith and being so disappointed in religion that I feel like throwing my hands up in defeat. *Please, God, I give up!* Some days I feel so frustrated, so angry, and so disheartened that if I hear one more homophobic, hypocritical, judgmental, mean-spirited, all-knowing, egotistical, ignorant comment made in the name of religion, I think I might lose my lunch into a toilet filled with holy water.

But through the discontent, the disappointments, and the disenchantment, there is a quiet, steady voice calling me, reassuring me, and telling me everything will be okay. It is God's voice made clear in the chirping birds and a warm April morning, a phone call from a dear friend, and my children's laughter. It is God's expansive hand reaching for my own small hand when my husband caresses my face, when I tuck my children into bed at night, and when my dad kisses my cheek. God is there in it all, and the peace I have found in an authentic faith wraps around me like a warm fleece blanket.

At the heart of my years of pretending and hiding, and my proclamations of inherited belief and massage therapy plans, was fear. There are two kinds of fear, I think. There is fear with the angry black wolf's face in the Dr. Seuss book *My Many Colored Days*. That's the fear of failure and embarrassment, of heartbreak and disappointment, and of doubt and pain. It tells us we aren't good enough, aren't worthy, and aren't beloved just as we are.

But then there is the other kind of fear, a slippery and sly kind of fear. It is a fear of that tiny little gem at the bottom of the Belief Gap that twinkles like the stars and shines like the sun. As Marianne Williamson wrote, "Our deepest fear is not that we are inadequate. Our deepest fear is that we are powerful beyond measure. It is our light, not our darkness, that most frightens us."[11]

It is this fear of the light within—a fear of the inherent goodness and the capacity to love—that keeps us from knowing and understanding ourselves. And it was a fear of real and true connection with people, with God, and with myself that scared me the most, and still scares me to this day. It is this fear that kept me from an authentic faith. It is this fear that caused me to initially hold Matt at arm's length, to keep him at a distance with a cast of characters and personas that might give me a slight upper hand and keep his soul from knowing mine.

It is this fear of sacred connection, of its blinding light and overwhelming power, that has been responsible for every ounce of inauthenticity in my life. All the "I love you's" that have gone unsaid. All the times I've wanted to eat just one more chocolate chip cookie fresh out of the oven, slightly undercooked, still warm and melty, but shamed myself out of it. All the times I've longed to

---

[11] Marianne Williamson, *A Return to Love*, (New York: Riverhead Books, 2002), 165.

run into my husband's arms when he gets home at the end of the day, tail-wagging and panting like the dogs do, but instead calling sedately, "Hi, honey, we're in the kitchen." All the times I've needed to bury my head into my mom's shoulder when the hurt, pain, and disappointment got too bad, but instead put on my best "I'll be okay" face. All the times I've prayed to a God I didn't believe in instead of praying to a God I do believe in. All the times I've wanted to wear a bikini and let my stomach pooch forward instead of sucking in my gut in that way that makes us feel like we are constantly out of breath. All the times I've prevented myself from loving and being loved fully and completely. All the times that I've wrapped my heart in duct tape to keep it from cracking open to the relentless grace and mercy.

So now I'm asking myself some new questions. Am I afraid of what might happen if my heart cracks open just a little? Am I afraid it might get broken, or that it will be cracked open, making a space for a kind of love and connection beyond anything I've experienced before? Am I afraid of getting hurt if I fall into a Belief Gap, or am I afraid of that twinkly, too-bright nugget of light that lies at the bottom? Am I hesitant to let myself be emotionally vulnerable because of the risk of disappointment and pain, or because of the potential for sacred connection that might come along with that nakedness? Am I scared of being hurt, or am I afraid of being opened up?

Brené Brown, a highly regarded expert on vulnerability and authenticity, said, "Embracing our vulnerabilities is risky but not nearly as dangerous as giving up on love and belonging and joy— the experiences that make us the most vulnerable. Only when we are brave enough to explore the darkness will we discover the infinite power of our light."[12]

---

[12] Brené Brown, *The Gifts of Imperfection: Let Go of Who You Think You're Supposed to Be and Embrace Who You Are*, (Center City: Hazeldon, 2010), 6.

It is impossible, I think, to "explore the darkness" as Brown recommends or acknowledge that we are "powerful beyond measure," as Marianne Williamson tells us, unless we first *know* ourselves. But how do we do that? How do we quiet all the noise and the roles we are told to fill and move beyond all the expectations others set for us? How do we stop giving others a version of us that we think they want and, instead, give them all of the *real* us?

These are tough questions and sticky issues, with no clear answers, of course. But, for me, I have found that it is easier to get to know the *real* me when I slowly peel away all expectations and assumptions. Like pulling back the rind of an orange, sometimes the pieces fall away in big chucks with great revelation and personal insight; other times, the rind is sticky and comes off in tiny orange flakes that just make a big mess. Sometimes, peeling back the layers leaves lots of that white stringy stuff that gets in our teeth and tastes horribly bitter. The peeling is a slow, sometimes painful, process. But it always leaves the sweet and juicy heart. It always leaves the real me, the grace-filled me, the *me* that I am meant to be.

Sometimes I need to peel, and sometimes I just need to jump. Sometimes I need to let myself fall off the cliff into the Belief Gap, leaving aside everything I had once thought I knew and all the ways I had known. I need to trust that the light and truth at the bottom will guide my way, and that something or someone will give me a parachute on the way down.

Because with each slow peel or each anxious leap, we are opening hearts, not the least of which is our own, so we can untangle knots and lift lids and open boxes, so we can be light-spreaders, connection-seekers, and grace-believers.

Dish Washing and Snow Shoveling

"Mindfulness is about love and loving life."
—Jon Kabat-Zinn

In a small town in central Wisconsin, my parents have a cottage on a tiny lake that feeds into a much larger one. The cottage has been in my mom's family for generations. When I was a child, my parents would bring my brother, sister, and me to the cottage almost every summer weekend.

Everything about the cottage is humble and understated. The only luxuries are the whirlpool bathtub and cable television. And the lake view, of course. Yet despite its no-frills appearance, the cottage is soft and cozy. Inside the front door, an umbrella stand holds a handful of old canes but surprisingly few (if any) umbrellas. A wooden bench holds towels and sandals. The bedroom closets are lined with blankets and pillows.

The kitchen is a place of function, with a modest stove, a small microwave, a fridge, and more than enough glasses to hold lemonade, iced tea, wine, or whiskey. While the cottage has kept up with technology in several respects—high-definition cable so my dad can watch the Brewers, Wi-Fi Internet so iPhones and iPads don't get neglected, and portable music speakers so I can play my latest favorite playlist—the cottage still lacks a dishwasher. And for this, I am utterly and eternally grateful.

Last summer, during one of our lay-led church services, someone read a passage by Thích Nhất Hạnh about washing dishes. I don't remember the precise words, but in general, the message was this: There are two ways to wash dishes. One way is to wash dishes to get clean dishes. The other way is to wash dishes to *wash dishes*.

When I'm at home, I will be the first to admit that I wash dishes for the sole purpose of cleaning the dishes. The task is annoying and time-consuming and leaves my hands wrinkled and dry. But, for some reason, when I am at the cottage, I wash dishes to *wash dishes*.

There is this natural tendency—one that is fed and fueled by societal expectations, I suppose—that tells us productivity must result in a finished product. The end matters more than the means. These messages begin at a very young age and continue throughout our lives, with tests scores, final exams, class rankings, job promotions, salary figures, and bigger homes. The finished result becomes the measuring stick, not the journey along the way.

We tell ourselves that *when* such-and-such happens, *then* we'll be happy. When we get married, when we have a baby, when the kids are in school, when the kids are out of the house, when we get the job, when we get the promotion, when we are out of debt, when we buy a house, when we get an agent, when we get published, when we receive this award, when we land that sales account, when the dishes are clean . . . *then* we'll be happy.

A few weeks ago, on a bitterly cold January afternoon, Matt and I were absolutely desperate to get out of the house so we took the boys bowling. Although Matt had taken Jackson, our seven year old, bowling a few times, this was the first time Teddy had been bowling. You can probably imagine how bowling with a four-year-old played out. For ten frames, Teddy grabbed his ball, stepped up to the line, and heaved the ball as hard as he could down the lane. Most of the time, he rolled the ball right into one of the bumpers and it would *sloooooowwwwly* bounce its way back and forth down the lane. On each of his rolls, the ball moved so slowly that I was pretty sure it wouldn't actually make it to the pins.

It was a bit unsettling at first, waiting so long and wondering whether the ball would actually make it to the end of the lane, but after a few frames, I realized the ball would *eventually* make it to the pins and that the real joy of bowling didn't come from knocking down pins but in what had happened while the ball was rolling. With the ball moving so slowly, I had time to soak it all in. I watched Teddy's eyes light up as the ball bounced down the lane, I stole a few glances at my husband, and I watched Jackson add up the scores on the screen. I couldn't tell you any of the scores from that game, but I will never forget the goings-on while the game was played. The real joy came in the ball-rolling, not the pin-knocking.

Sometimes the ball of life moves just as slowly. Infinitely more slowly than we'd like. We watch the ball roll and bounce and chug along. We dip dish after dish into soapy water. We wait and wait and wait, always with an eye toward the knocked-down pins and the clean dishes. But while holding an eagle-eye view on the end-result—the score, the finished project, the promotion, the book deal, the bigger house—we run the risk of missing all that's going on while we're waiting, while we're washing our dishes and rolling bowling balls.

We miss the twinkly eyes and the subtle emotions, the learning and the growing, the graceful movement to it all, the sights and sounds and people and various goings-on that are actually a really big deal if we'd just stop focusing so much on the pins at the end of the lane and the need for clean dishes on the counter.

The antidote for all this antsy waiting for the Next Big Thing and rushed movement to the End Result is no secret and it's nothing new: Mindfulness. Paying attention. Being aware. Washing dishes for the sake of washing dishes.

Thích Nhất Hạnh, the great Buddhist teacher, has much to say about the importance of mindfulness, particularly when doing routine chores and everyday tasks. For instance, of washing dishes, he says:

To my mind, the idea that doing dishes is unpleasant can occur only when you aren't doing them. Once you are standing in front of the sink with your sleeves rolled up and your hands in the warm water, it is really quite pleasant. I enjoy taking my time with each dish, being fully aware of the dish, the water, and each movement of my hands. I know that if I hurry in order to eat dessert sooner, the time of washing dishes will be unpleasant and not worth living. That would be a pity, for each minute, each second of life is a miracle. The dishes themselves and that fact that I am here washing them are miracles![13]

But while the antidote might be straight forward, that doesn't necessarily mean that it's an easy one to implement. There is a natural tendency (especially for us impatient Type A's) to rush through daily chores, to focus on project completion and checking things off the to-do list, and to prioritize the marks of productivity instead of the journey. The trouble is that these are the very things that make up our lives. As an at-home mom with two young children, so much of my day is filled with tedium and tasks that are the epitome of unproductivity—making meals and cleaning up after meals, filling cups with juice and soaking up spills with paper towels, washing clothes that will be dirtied again the next day, picking up toys that will be scattered about in mere moments, bringing in the mail, paying bills, and shuffling children from one activity to the next—all before collapsing in bed at the end of the day.

For those who work outside the home, time is also filled with routine chores and never-ending projects: spreadsheets,

---

[13] Thích Nhất Hạnh, "Bathing a Newborn Buddha" in *Next to Godliness: Finding the Sacred in Housekeeping*, ed. by Alice Peck, (Woodstock: Skylight Paths Publishing, 2007), 3.

unanswered e-mails, conference calls, letters to be sent and letters to be answered, reports to be submitted, nails to be hammered, coffee to be poured, papers to be graded.

The vast majority of our days, weeks, months, and years are just a series of little moments. But it is all of these tiny moments and seemingly ordinary goings-on that matter; it is in each and every one of these small things that we find the big things: grace, connection, joy.

There is grace in caring for the needs of another human being, whether a child who needs a Band-Aid and a hug, a co-worker who needs help with a project, a parent who needs more frequent phone calls, a spouse who needs dry cleaning picked up, or a friend who could use some fresh-baked cookies. There is spiritual fulfillment and sacred connection in caring for others, for ourselves, for our homes, and for our communities. There is love at the bottom of a pile of laundry. There is joy in watching the bowling ball roll. There is affection in a sizzling pan of stir-fried vegetables. And there is grace in the sudsy bubbles of a sink full of dishes.

Mindfulness is not to be confused, however, with enjoyment. It's a common misconception that to be mindful and aware we must feel happy and content in the moment. But practicing mindfulness doesn't mean we must ignore the discomfort or sadness or cruelty of the present moment any more than we need to pretend that our hands aren't wet and wrinkly while we're washing the dishes.

Thích Nhất Hạnh also writes:

Feelings, whether of compassion or irritation, should be welcomed, recognized, and treated on an absolutely equal basis; because both are ourselves. The tangerine I am eating is me. The mustard greens I am planting are me. I plant with all my heart and mind. I clean this teapot with the kind of attention I would have were I giving the baby

41

Buddha or Jesus a bath. Nothing should be treated more carefully than anything else. In mindfulness, compassion, irritation, mustard green plant, and teapot are all sacred.[14]

Washing dishes is wet, bowling with a four-year-old is slow, and cleaning toilets is unpleasant. Shoveling snow is cold, backbreaking work. Preparing spreadsheets is mind numbing, and toddler tantrums at the grocery store are embarrassing and frustrating. To be mindful, present, and aware does not mean we need to pretend that it isn't cold or boring or frustrating; mindfulness only asks that we give these activities—along with the people affected by these activities and our feelings while doing these activities—our full and complete attention.

Mindfulness is a difficult concept for me to grasp; my mind likes to jump from one thing to the next and focus on the completion rather than the process. But like all spiritual practices, mindfulness takes repetition, effort, and . . . well . . . *practice.* To be aware, to appreciate the means and not just the end, and to be mindful of the potential for sacred connection, we need to practice for the sake of rolling balls and not for the sake of knocking down pins. We need to practice washing dishes for the sake of washing dishes and not for the sake of clean dishes.

We need to practice. Let our minds wander now and then. And then practice some more.

The practice of mindfulness—washing dishes for the sake of washing dishes—is really a practice in grace. It is a practice in living fully and connecting deeply. It is a practice in opening boxes. Because like washing dishes and laundry folding, spreadsheets and bill paying, the real connection comes in the small, ordinary,

---

[14] Thích Nhất Hạnh, *The Miracle of Mindfulness: An Introduction to the Practice of Meditation,* (Boston: Beacon Press, 1975), 61.

repetitive, and seemingly lackluster moments that make up our days, years, and lives.

Opening boxes (whether literally or figuratively) happens one corner at a time, often in slow and clumsy movements. Connection happens the same way, too, sometimes. A glass of wine poured for our spouse at the end of a long day. Clean clothes folded and placed in drawers for our children. Dry cleaning picked up, meals cooked, dishes washed and put away. So often we do these things on autopilot without much thought, and if we do pay them any mind, it is usually to bemoan the task (or the recipients thereof).

But by paying attention—feeling the softness of the fabric as we fold laundry, seeing the sunlight reflected on the suds as we wash dishes, thinking affectionately of our spouse as we pick up the tossed-aside socks for the *millionth time*—we connect with ourselves and our thoughts, the world around us and the people in it. Not in some dramatic and obvious way, but perhaps in a more subtle, sustainable, and meaningful way.

So I'm practicing this mindfulness thing that comes so unnaturally to me. I practice when I'm elbow deep in a soapy sink filled with dirty dishes. I practice when I watch the bowling ball bounce ever so slowly down the lane, when I'm sorting socks and making lunches, and when I'm cleaning crumbs between the couch cushions. I practice when I'm spreading peanut butter, seeing little ones safely off to school, and answering pesky client e-mails. I practice mindfulness and awareness.

Except when I'm scrubbing the toilets. It's still hard for me to see anything other than germs, much less grace, in that one. Maybe with some more practice, I will eventually be able to find the grace in cleaning toilets too.

Heck, if I can learn to find the grace and purpose in washing dishes anything is possible.

Letting Go While Holding On

"Some of us think holding on makes us strong;
but sometimes it is letting go."
—Hermann Hesse

For me, the process of creating a written piece of work consists largely of two parts: the building up and the letting go. Or in other words, the writing and the editing.

It's hard to say which one—the writing or the editing—is more difficult. My mood, my energy level, whether I have had one cup of coffee or two, and even the weather can impact the level of my enthusiasm and the degree of difficulty I attach to each phase.

Sometimes, filling a blank page with a collection of words and phrases that resemble anything close to a coherent idea, let alone an entertaining or inspiring idea, seems like the most daunting task imaginable. Like climbing Everest or swimming the English Channel or running a marathon.

Or driving cross-country in a minivan with two toddlers.

The building-up phase of the process is messy and chaotic, perhaps disjointed and jumpy, but it is uninhibited and limitless. Some days it's like opening the lawn spigot at the end of a long winter. After you turn the knob, nothing happens for a while, then slowly a few drops of water trickle out and eventually the water is flowing freely. Similarly, I sit down, turn on the computer, and wait for the words to come. I spend a lot of time staring at my computer screen, checking Facebook, and e-mailing my husband about weekend plans even though it's only Monday morning. I slowly tap out a few clumsy sentences about who knows what, and eventually the keys are *clickety-clacking* away. Before long, I've filled up a page, then two, then three, and my fingers can barely keep up with the thoughts spilling onto the page.

Other days, the spigot never turns. It's frozen, stuck, and immovable. These are the days when I know that it's best just to move on to something else, like cleaning the fridge, walking the dogs, or reading a favorite book.

The other part of the process—the editing—is similarly temperamental. I think what makes the editing part so hard, painful even, is that at its core, it is about figuring out what to let go of and what to hold on to. That's no simple task in the writing process, or in life for that matter.

When I first began writing with the goal of creating something akin to a book, I asked a few close friends and trusted spiritual advisors to read the manuscript. Some of the initial readers spotted typos, while others pointed out paragraphs that needed a little more "meat on the bones," as they say. And one friend suggested that the entire book be reworked, molded differently, and refocused in a more coherent way. When she first told me that the manuscript felt disjointed, like it was two different books written under the same name, I wanted to crawl under the covers and cry. She was, of course, right with every aspect of her assessment. The manuscript *was* disjointed, unfocused, and a bit flat. I just didn't want to hear all these things because I needed to let go of so much to incorporate the necessary changes and make the manuscript better, and to tell the story that I was really trying to tell.

The thought of sifting through all these words and thoughts and ideas I had so painstakingly worked to create seemed utterly impossible. I suppose that's why a good editor is worth his or her weight in gold. Nonetheless, I spent days and weeks slashing, cutting, and letting go, keeping only the essential components.

A good piece of editing advice is to cut anything that doesn't advance the story. The same, I would suggest, is true with life and our spiritual journey. Cut anything that doesn't advance your story.

Easier said than done, I suppose. How do we know what advances the story so we can decide what to let go of and what to hold on to? It is no easy task. In fact, the art of letting go and holding on may be the essence of one's lifelong spiritual path.

Part of what draws me into the writing process is that it so closely mirrors life. There are days when the words float rather easily onto the page, when the building up and assembling of sentences and paragraphs seems to come almost naturally, as if my hands are simply fulfilling the purpose to which they were called to do. And, similarly, in my day-to-day life, there are days that unfold freely and easily, mornings when I get the kids to school on time without screaming, "Hurry up! We're gonna be late!" Days when I have a productive morning with few distractions, when I get a few errands done without any embarrassing tantrums, when I have a few minutes to have a late afternoon glass of wine with a friend while our kids play spies and Star Wars, and when Matt and I chat breezily about this and that. There are days when I feel connected, energized, and full.

And then there are days when I feel stuck. When the words get caught somewhere between my head and my fingertips, or they lay motionless in my brain. There are days when the kids don't want to get dressed in the morning, when nothing on the to-do list is accomplished, when I have a snippy and somewhat hostile e-mail exchange with a friend or family member, or when Matt and I are communicating at different wavelengths and with different radio frequencies. Days when I feel stuck and immobile, like I'm jogging slowly but painfully on the treadmill of life while everyone else speeds past me with a bright smile and a water bottle in hand.

And just like it is hard to know what to cut and what to keep to advance a literary story, it's also difficult to know what to let go of and what to hold on to in this work of art we call Life. Nonetheless, we remain in this constant, perpetual cycle of building up, letting go, and holding on. The key, I suppose, is knowing *when* to build up, *when* to let go, and *when* to hold on, and then having the courage to do so.

In *The Gift of an Ordinary Day*, Katrina Kenison writes about her parenting journey from a mother of two teenage boys to an empty nester over the course of just a few years. She describes coming to terms with her sons leaving home and heading off to college, and her new role as a mother to adults and the drastically changed routine of her daily life. She writes of letting go of childhood and a certain way of life, and holding on to family and the perpetually changing nature of life. "There is indeed an art to it, this fine mingling of letting go and holding on," she says.[15]

An art, a struggle, a quest. In whatever way you think of letting go and holding on, there must be a balance between the two. What that balance is, I'm not entirely sure, but I'm wondering if the key might be to hold on to love and hope while being able to let go of just about everything else.

Parker Palmer wrote in *A Hidden Wholeness: The Journey Toward an Undivided Life*, "The deeper our faith, the more doubt we must endure; the deeper our hope, the more prone we are to despair; the deeper our love, the more pain its loss will bring: these are a few of the paradoxes we must hold as human beings. If we refuse to hold them in the hopes of living without doubt, despair, and pain, we also find ourselves living without faith, hope, and love."[16]

---

[15] Katrina Kenison, *The Gift of an Ordinary Day*, (New York: Springboard Press, 2009), 245.
[16] Parker Palmer, *A Hidden Wholeness: The Journey Toward an Undivided Life*, Parker Palmer, (San Francisco: Jossey-Bass, 2004), 82–83.

We are afraid of the pain that comes with the eventual letting go, so we don't hold on. And yet we must hold on to love and hope—and faith, as Palmer suggests—if we are to have any chance at spiritual connection.

There is an intense fear of losing love, pleasantness, and the familiar, of course, but I think that on a deeper level there is also a hidden fear of losing some of the anger and negativity as well. Over the course of my nearly four decades of life, I have been hurt in some spectacular and truly abhorrent ways. Like many of us, I am no stranger to deceit, betrayal, and devastating rejection. The pain that these experiences caused were, without a doubt, among some of the most agonizing and raw experiences I have endured—*at that time*. But like the cut of a sharp knife, once the cut healed, I let go of the pain relatively easily. These devastating, horrific misdeeds do not keep me up at night, nor do I spend time plotting revenge or ruminating on all of the ways I was wronged. For the most part, I have let these transgressions go.

But it is the minor indiscretions (both mine and those of others) that are harder to let go. It is the snippy, rude comments, the shortcomings, the differences of opinion, the expectations that fell short, the unspoken apologies, and the times when I feel taken for granted. The emotional abrasions that rub and chafe and never fully heal . . . those things are more difficult to let go.

Letting go of the pain and disappointments, especially when it comes from someone we care about deeply or when we are the ones causing the pain to someone we care about, is difficult for a couple of reasons. First, these everyday emotional abrasions often go unaddressed. There are no obscenities hurled, no raised voices, no slammed doors, and no verbal exorcism of the pain and hostility that lingers inside. So the hurt, pain, and anger are left to linger and grow.

Second, I think that the emotional abrasions are more difficult to heal than the deep emotional cuts because they force us to confront and then accept our flawed and imperfect humanity. It can be easier to move on from one spectacular betrayal than to let go of the resentment caused when a friend forgets our birthday, our children disrespect us, or our spouse doesn't communicate with us. We tell ourselves that these things aren't that big of a deal, that we shouldn't feel bad, that we should just get over it. And then because we *do* feel bad and we *do* feel a little hurt, annoyed, and let down, we end up feeling bad about *ourselves* for feeling the way we do. And maybe even a little annoyed that we are now forced to confront our own emotional shortcomings.

The anger and pain become familiar, like a ratty old blanket we carried around as a child. To give up that anger and pain means we have to hold ourselves open and exposed to the elements. And this can be absolutely terrifying.

But what I am beginning to learn, slowly and clumsily, is that letting go of the disappointment and frustration—whether caused by a deep knife cut or an unhealed abrasion—is a spiritual practice, an intentional and committed decision. Letting go means we make the affirmative decision to honor a love for humanity and ourselves more than we honor the comfort we derive from the persistent anger and pain. Letting go means accepting that all of us are flawed and imperfect humans, that none of us is better or worse than the other, and that just as we have been hurt, so, too, have we hurt others.

Not only is it hard to let go of the pain and disappointment, but it is hard to let go of the expectations, the way we thought life should turn out, or the way we think others should act and behave and be. Parenting, I have found, just might be the ultimate act of letting go. It seems that from the moment those two pink lines appear on the stick, there is a constant letting go, or a need to let go. There's a letting go of clothes that no longer fit, of an old way of life, and of expectations for the ways things should turn out. And the letting go is amplified even more once that tiny little being takes his or her first breath or exuberant cry. We let go of a lifestyle, of preconceived ideas of what parenthood would look

50

like, and of a previous identity because from now on our identity will inextricably include that of "Mom" or "Dad."

As our children grow through various phases and milestones, each new door means a closing door as well. We let go of wrinkly newborns and squishy, toothless babies, of stumbling toddlers and strong-willed preschoolers, and of defiant tweens and headstrong teenagers. All the while, as we move on and let go, we mourn and grieve a little bit every step of the way.

One of my first great tests in letting go as a parent came when Jackson started first grade. Prior to that time, Jackson and I had spent the vast majority of his seven years together. When he was a baby and I was an awkward new mom, I joked that he was like a really cute purse (that cried) since I rarely went anywhere without him. Over the years, we became more like a co-dependent couple, sometimes driving each other mad with our constant togetherness, but always a little lost without each other, until we reached that point where he—an independent, energetic, and curious little boy—was no longer quite so lost without me.

Each day that I drop him off at school and watch his red backpack bob up and down as he runs to join his classmates, I taste the bittersweet tonic of budding independence and the tang of letting go. A few minutes later, having dropped off Teddy at preschool for a few hours, I tend to all those tasks that need tending, and I am grateful for those moments of freedom and uninterrupted hours to write, drink a cup of coffee, or e-mail a friend. But while I fold laundry, make work phone calls, and check things off my to-do list, I always wonder: *Does he know that not a minute goes by when he is not on my mind or in my heart? Does he know that my favorite part of the day is when he walks in the door, tossing his backpack on the floor, and calling out for a snack? Does he know that while he is away at school, learning and playing, there is a constant and mildly uncomfortable nagging feeling in my gut?* What I'm feeling is the slippery rope of his childhood sliding through my fingers. It is the subtle and constant pain of letting go.

But regardless of how uncomfortable letting go is, and regardless of how much I drag my feet through it like a petulant child, this season will end. My children will grow up and move away. We will move past these days of bedtimes and backpacks and skinned knees to days of curfews and car keys and broken hearts. We will move through, we will move on, and we will let go because that is, after all, what all of us are doing every minute of every day of every season: letting go. Always just letting go and moving on.

I suppose all we can hope for is a little bit of grace as we practice this delicate art of letting go. We all hope that something, or someone, is reaching out to us from the other side because letting go feels like the most *ungraceful* thing in the world sometimes. First, there is the clinging, the tightened grip on what is or was. Then there might be the denial, and a hint of defensiveness, that it's time to let go. Sometimes our grip loosens a little at a time until eventually we have let go; other times, our grip only subsides when our palms are raw and bloody from our too-tight grasp.

What I have found eases the pain of letting go is the reminder that when we let go of one thing, we are essentially freeing ourselves up to grab something else. We are lifting the lids off some tightly closed boxes—the ones locked up in chains disguised as safety and comfort—so that we can let what is inside breathe a little. And, in doing so, we also open some of the unopened and neglected boxes that have gone unnoticed until now. We open ourselves up to new opportunities, insights, and connections. We open ourselves up to possibility, and freeing ourselves to say "yes!" to all that life has to offer.

That Time I Quit the Swim Team

"Mistakes are always forgivable, if one has the courage to admit them."
—Bruce Lee

People are sometimes surprised to learn that my dad was my swimming coach for nearly ten years. If you are familiar with the sport of swimming, you know it is no casual spectator sport. Practices are long and grueling, with morning practices beginning well before dawn and another long practice after school. If practices weren't time-consuming and exhausting enough, swim meets are an even bigger test of one's endurance. Competitions are often a two- to three-day event, with warm-ups beginning at the first light of day and the meet continuing until well past dinnertime.

Swimming, in short, is not for the faint of heart. Yet, for some reason, when I was about eight years old, our swim team found itself without a coach and my dad agreed to step in. I'm sure he didn't know that when he agreed to coach this fledgling team in a small Wisconsin town, his tenure as coach would continue for nearly thirty years.

As the team grew, and my passion for swimming increased, my dad's involvement in the sport grew as well. He attended coaching conferences, read books on stroke technique, and spent hours planning practices, not to mention the time and energy he gave to the actual practices and competitions.

Having my dad as my coach took the typical parent-teen relationship and completely flipped it on its head. While other fathers might have been cautious and somewhat fearful around their teen daughters, my dad and I often talked about boys and dating, diet and menstrual cycles, sex and drinking, and confidence and humility. Given the amount of time we spent together, and the fact that many of my swimming successes were shared successes in a coach-athlete kind of way, our relationship was like a parent-child connection on steroids. He knew more about me than he might otherwise have known, and yet there was a certain boundary line that wasn't there due to the fact that he was parent, coach, mentor, and teacher all wrapped into one.

As a teen athlete I was especially dramatic and prone to theatrics, often stubborn and haughty, and yet deeply anxious and exhausted. As a coach, my father was many of these things as well, which created some rather volatile situations between the two of us. Like any parent and teen, there were fights and power struggles. But unlike most other parents and teens, these arguments were often on the pool deck in front of teammates and friends.

We had one argument that was especially bitter and divisive yet also infused with grace. I don't remember what started it or why things escalated, but it ended with him kicking me out of practice. "Just go," he said as ten pairs of eyes stared at me, wondering what I would do.

I was pretty sure at the time that he didn't really want me to go; he was just angry at me. But I was also absolutely certain that his response was unwarranted, dramatic, and absolutely humiliating.

I stormed off the pool deck, quickly changed in the locker room, and cried all the way home (which was only about five minutes away since we lived across the street from the practice pool).

"What happened?" my mom gasped when I stomped through the front door, slamming it hard behind me.

I told her the story, about how embarrassed I was, and that I couldn't handle having my dad as a coach. And then I told her that I was going to quit the swim team.

I knew that my dad hadn't meant what he said on the pool deck and he reacted out of anger, but I also knew that I wouldn't really quit. I was just angry and hurt.

Later that night, when we both had calmed down, my dad and I talked about what had happened and he apologized to me. I forgave him, but I was still tender and wounded. I didn't return to the swimming pool the next day or the day after that. I knew I needed to take a step back and reconsider the way swimming fit into my life and the way it was affecting my relationships. I needed to breathe and rest. But I also wanted to prove a point. I wanted just a touch of revenge for the embarrassment he had caused me. (And there might have been some histrionics and teen angst thrown in for good measure.)

Since I wasn't at practice the day after the argument, I didn't hear my dad apologize in front of a group of fifteen to twenty teenagers. I didn't hear him tell the wide-eyed youngsters, friends and acquaintances of mine, as well as younger swimmers who I suspect looked up to me, that he had overreacted, that he was wrong, and that he was sorry. I wasn't there to hear him tell them that I wouldn't be at practice for a few days, and that he understood and supported the reason for my break. I didn't see him stand in front of this group of teens, who looked to him for direction and answers, and confess that he had made a mistake, that he didn't always have the answers.

I didn't hear him say these things, but he said them.

There are many things about my father for which any daughter would be proud: he is a successful businessman and entrepreneur, a well-respected member of the community, an active volunteer, an affectionate husband, and a supportive and generous father and grandfather. But in spite of all of the attributes, accolades, and accomplishments, the courage that it took to admit his mistakes at the poolside and apologize with sincerity and humility, not just to me, but to a bunch of head-strong teenagers, is the thing of which I am most proud about my dad to this day.

How much easier would it have been to say nothing at all? To return to business as usual, wielding his whistle and stopwatch, as if nothing had happened? Or how much easier would it have been to defend his position, reiterating that disrespect and hostile attitudes had no place on the pool deck?

Certainly, there are a number of different paths my father could have taken after the argument, many of which would have been understandable and justified. Instead, he chose the path of grace and humility and surrender. He chose the path of connection.

We like to think of grace as an art form, a moving through life with quiet ease. But grace isn't moving through life smoothly, gliding and twirling like a ballerina; grace is a jumpy and haphazard polka, hot and sweaty, as we step on our partners' toes and bump into our fellow dancers. Grace isn't floating on calm waters in one of those large inflatable rafts with cup holders and head rests; grace is surviving in choppy, white-capped waters with only an orange life preserver to keep you afloat.

Grace isn't moving through life mistake-free, or always saying what's right and doing what's right; grace is mucking things up and then having the courage to ineloquently say, "I'm sorry, I was wrong, and I'd like to make this right."

And grace is saying, "I know, I forgive you." And meaning it.

Wet and Heavy T-Shirts

"When we were children, we used to think that when we were grown-up we would no longer be vulnerable. But to grow up is to accept vulnerability . . .
To be alive is to be vulnerable."
—Madeleine L'Engle

Each spring, schools across the country mark the impending departure of graduating students with some kind of class trip. In our large suburban town, the fifth graders take a hiking trip to southern Wisconsin. A neighboring suburb's eighth-grade class takes an overnight trip to Springfield, our state capital. Nearly twenty-five years ago, when I was about to move on from the quiet halls of middle school to the rambling maze of high school, our eighth-grade class took a day trip to a waterpark in Wisconsin Dells.

Wisconsin Dells is a kind of Midwestern Vegas minus the clinking slot machines, the posh resorts, the lux shopping, and the stadium-seating show venues. The Dells is gaudy, brash, and assaulting to the senses in every possible way, and I loved every bit of it.

The outdoor waterpark Noah's Ark was my absolute favorite part of the Dells. It's filled with fast-moving rides like the Plunge, long, winding channels of water like the Endless River, and undulating wave pools like the Big Kahuna. Each day leading up to our class trip was met with increasing jittery excitement and nagging apprehension. High schools and middle schools operate with a political system all their own, especially in a town as small as the one where I grew up. Cliques were drawn with thick black lines, using rules and standards I never seemed to be able to understand or was always a half-step behind. The rules for fitting in were difficult to comprehend and were constantly changing. Stone-washed jeans rolled at the bottom were a fashion necessity one day, and the next day they would earn you a spot on the list of fashion misfits. Bands and popular music changed with the seasons, and since our family didn't have cable television, I couldn't rely on MTV to stay in the know.

Because I was always a half-step behind, I spent a lot of time watching and noticing. I paid attention to what the cool girls wore and how they did their hair. I noticed how the boys looked at certain girls, and the way gaggles of girls crowded around the same lockers between classes, talking with their heads close together, and giggling in unison. I paid attention to the swift and senseless way someone could quickly go from being "in" to being "out."

All this is to say, I suppose, that in middle school (and for several years thereafter) I did a whole lot of following and not much listening to that squirmy little voice inside.

While I was usually a few steps behind the "cool curve," I felt fairly confident and eager going into the eighth-grade class trip. I had been on the swim team for about seven years at that point, so I felt comfortable in and around the water. Plus, I had a really cool new swimming suit—a mock two-piece that tied at the hips that I couldn't wait to show off. *Finally,* I thought, *I know the rules and I can fit in.*

After a raucous and bumpy ninety-minute bus ride, our group of a hundred rowdy tweens and a handful of tired teachers arrived at the waterpark. Groups broke off—boys going in one direction, girls in the other—to change in the locker rooms before reuniting with tingly teen hormones.

I trailed behind the group of girls I called "friends," following them into the locker room. They each went into a private changing room, so I did the same. I pulled on my new and oh-so-awesome swimsuit and smiled at myself in the mirror. *Wow, cool suit, Christie,* they would say. *Where'd you get it?* they'd ask in envy. *Come down the slide with us, Christie,* the boys would call out.

I stepped out from behind the curtain and waited for the compliments to start pouring in, eager for a chance to finally feel like I was "in" instead of constantly lagging behind. But when the curtains beside me opened and the other girls stepped out, I realized that once again the rules had changed, catching me completely off-guard. I stood there dazed and confused as the other girls, wearing big, baggy T-shirts over their suits, preened themselves in the mirror.

Having spent the majority of my afterschool hours in the swimming pool training and competing, it hadn't even dawned on me that a person might wear a T-shirt *over* her swimming suit *while in the water.* The only T-shirt I had was an old, dingy white shirt that was far too short to accomplish the desired effect.

I guess this will have to do, I thought with a defeated sigh, though the idea of wearing a T-shirt over my cute new suit seemed absolutely absurd to me. I put on the T-shirt and joined the other girls, knowing again that I was a half-step behind.

Although hiding under a bulky, uncomfortable T-shirt didn't make sense to me, I knew enough to know that if I wanted to stand a chance at fitting in, I needed to hide under whatever T-shirt I could find and suffer the discomfort that came with it. I knew if I were uncovered and exposed (albeit in a tasteful swimsuit at a waterpark), that I would be different, I wouldn't fit in, and I might not belong. So for the rest of the day, I plunged down steep waterslides, mastered the waves in the big pool, and floated in inner tubes down the lazy river. All with a hot, wet, sticky T-shirt clinging to me.

Late in the afternoon, just an hour before we needed to load the buses to get home, a group of classmates and I floated around the lazy river. Boys splashed and dunked each other under the water. Girls giggled and pretended to be annoyed. With each lap around the lazy river, I grew more and more annoyed with this wet T-shirt that lay like an albatross around my shoulders.

The thing about wet, sticky T-shirts is that they eventually become just too heavy a burden to bear. The discomfort of covering up outweighs the potential discomfort of being exposed. So with an hour left in our day at the waterpark, I looked around at the group of covered-up girls, who all looked the same in some kind of desperate attempt to cover up any perceived flaws and hide their changing bodies. I looked down at my own T-shirt, clinging awkwardly to my flat chest, and realized that the price of covering up was much too high.

So I tore off the shirt and sank into the cool liquid, relishing the water's velvety touch. I emerged and stretched my scrawny thirteen-year-old body across an inner tube and just floated for a while. No one said anything, but I caught a few suspicious looks pass between some of the girls.

I don't remember much about that class trip. I don't remember the bus ride to the waterpark or the bus ride home. I couldn't tell you what rides we went on or who was flirting with whom. I don't know which boy I had a crush on at the time or where we ate for lunch. I don't remember which girls were fighting or whether anyone got in trouble for smoking or making out on the bus. What I do remember is the discomfort that came with covering up in the wet and heavy T-shirt, and the liberation I felt when I finally tore it off and stopped hiding.

That evening, after the bus pulled into the school parking lot and I had said good-bye to a few friends with promises to keep in touch over the summer, I walked home with an odd mixture of pride and freedom, as well as a prickly feeling of dread. *What have I done? What will people think of me now that they've seen me uncovered and exposed?*

I have learned over the years that what I had felt that day is the prickliness of vulnerability. It's kind of like a sunburn after a long day at the beach, or a skinned knee after falling off your bike.

The prickliness of vulnerability is a touch of pain accompanied by the feeling of freedom that comes from having done something truly authentic, personal, and unabashed.

The pain isn't unbearable, but just uncomfortable enough that we turn away from it. We cover up.

But what if we were to welcome the discomfort instead of covering it up? What if we were to hold our breath, grit our teeth, and give ourselves a chance to get comfortable with the discomfort?

Would we adjust?

Would we learn?

Would we grow?

Would we feel free and light and hopeful?

Would we feel peaceful and calm?

Would we feel a greater sense of connection?

The idea that exposing ourselves—whether it's loving someone fully and completely, living a truly authentic life, admitting our fears and insecurities, or confessing our flaws and weaknesses—could potentially lead to sacred connection seems almost counterintuitive at times. If we love someone fully and completely, what happens if the love isn't returned, or it fades, or that person leaves us by choice or in death? If we admit our flaws and insecurities, aren't we putting ourselves at risk of being taken advantage of? If we confess our flaws and weaknesses, won't others be turned off by our imperfections? These risks are very real. Love might be lost, and some people might take advantage of us or be turned off. But these risks can be managed with wise, instinctual, and careful decisions about who to trust and how we let ourselves be exposed and unprotected.

Brené Brown talks about the willingness to be exposed and unprotected as an act of courage and bravery. "Heroics," she writes, "is often about putting our life on the line. Ordinary courage is about putting our *vulnerability* on the line."[17]

Many of us cover up to avoid being exposed and unprotected in an attempt to fit in and belong. We think we can hide our differences and assimilate by covering up. Brown describes the differences like this: "Fitting in is about assessing a situation and becoming who you need to be to be accepted. Belonging, on the other hand, doesn't require us to *change* who we are; it requires us to *be* who we are."[18]

By looking and acting like everyone else, we can fit in. And when we fit in, we tell ourselves we belong. But fitting in and belonging are two very different things.

Fitting in is a behavior. Belonging is a state of being.

Fitting in is simulation. Belonging is connection.

Fitting in is closing boxes. Belonging is opening them.

Fitting in is covering up under wet and sticky T-shirts. Belonging is flaunting a mock two-piece swimsuit with ties at the sides.

---

[17] Brown, *The Gifts of Imperfection*, 13.
[18] Brown, *The Gifts of Imperfection*, 25.

Hablas Español?

"True hospitality is marked by an open response to the dignity of each and every person."
—Kathleen Norris

After Jackson, my oldest son, was born, I developed a passion for entertaining. Since we were the only ones in our Chicago group of friends with a baby, hosting small gatherings was the easiest way for Matt and me to carry on some kind of social life. Given that the vast majority of our close friends at the time were single men, most Saturday evenings consisted of dinner and cocktails until midnight or so when Matt and I, the perpetually overtired parents, would drag ourselves to bed, and our childless friends would head out to flirt with girls at one of the many neighborhood bars.

Hosting dinner parties also became my favorite hobby for the sense of purpose it gave my week. On Monday or Tuesday, I would e-mail a few friends to check on availability. Wednesday and Thursday would be spent planning the menu, poring over cookbooks, and surfing the web for new ideas. Friday would be grocery shopping. Saturday would be filled with preparations— cutting and chopping, roasting and sautéing—while Jackson napped or curiously watched from his baby seat. The table would be set, bottles of wine and whiskey would be pulled out of the cabinet above the fridge, and iPod playlists would be chosen.

I am no Martha Stewart when it comes to entertaining, but I have no doubt that fifty years from now I will look back on those Saturday nights—when a handful of friends crowded around our tiny table in our shoebox-sized kitchen, talking and laughing—

as some of the most satisfying nights of my life. These gatherings provided a kind of escape from the realities of life and a way to bring the outside world into our sheltered cocoon for a few hours. There is something almost magical about a collection of beloved guests, friends gathered around a table, bellies and hearts full, candles flickering, and music playing.

Inevitably, however, most of these gatherings included at least one or two unintended guests. Someone who had initially declined changed his mind at the last minute. Acquaintances who happened to be in the neighborhood. Friends of friends who heard that food was being served. New girlfriends and out-of-town guests. And just as inevitable as the uninvited guests, so too was the frustration it caused me.

I'd stew and balk. "We don't have enough food," I'd moan to Matt.

"Yes, we do," he would say.

"We don't have enough room," I'd lament.

"I'll bring up some extra chairs," he would offer.

"How rude," I'd grumble.

"Yes, how rude," Matt would agree, though it took me a few years to realize that he was talking about *me*, not them.

True hospitality isn't about RSVPs and enough chairs and matching wineglasses. Hospitality, at its core, is really about one thing: an open and welcoming spirit. Hospitality, I have learned, is not the same as entertaining, and yet all too often, in our Pinterest and Martha Stewart culture, we tend to confuse the two. Entertaining is about offering up amusement, and holding others captive with a sense of pleasure. Conversely, hospitality is about creating a space into which the guest, stranger, family, or friend can enter and simply be welcome and at ease. In fact, the meaning of the word *hospitality* comes from two Greek words, one that means "love," and the other that means "strangers." In other words, hospitality is "love of strangers," not entertainment of guests. When hospitality focuses on loving strangers, on creating a space where people can enter as they are and feel welcome, it has the ability to connect and bind in transformative and miraculous ways.

If we are to practice true hospitality in a way that creates sacred connection, we must welcome everyone—not just invited guests, but the uninvited and the strangers—with an expansive openness and the spirit of inclusivity such that all who cross the threshold of our homes, neighborhoods, communities, and our country feel welcome.

When we bought our house five years ago, we knew it would need a significant amount of renovation. The kitchen had not been updated since 1975, the family room was small and drafty, and the basement guest bedroom felt a little more akin to a prison cell than a guest room. Over the course of a few years, we hired contractors to help with these projects. For months at a time, a team of Spanish-speaking young men worked in and around our home. They were privy to toddler tantrums and potty-training little boys. They heard a baby's cries and a mom's desperate pleas to *shhhhh* while they tore down walls and built up new ones, hammered and nailed, spackled and painted, varnished and stained. And in many ways through their efforts, over the past several years we were able to convert an old house into our home.

The team's leader, Gilbert, spoke both English and Spanish, but the rest of his team spoke only Spanish. Consequently, whenever I had a question for one of the non-English-speaking workers, I spoke with Gilbert and he would interpret from English to Spanish and back again. On those rare occasions when Gilbert was tending to a job at another location, I would need to communicate directly with a Spanish-speaking worker. I would ask a question in English in the hopes that he might understand. I would point and gesture. He would stumble a few words of English and gesture back. We communicated clumsily, but effectively.

This kind of situation might seem like nothing out of the ordinary. Certainly, individuals across the country have been overcoming linguistic barriers and cultural divides to communicate since the beginning of time. But my story has a sad and shameful twist: I actually know a little Spanish.

To be entirely truthful, I majored in Spanish in college.

"Why didn't you just speak Spanish?" you might be asking. A fair question to be sure, with a simple—albeit inexcusable—answer: embarrassment and fear. I have not spoken Spanish for more than fifteen years, and I don't remember much anymore. Even at the height of my familiarity with the language, I wasn't what you would consider fluent. Speaking Spanish was awkward and difficult; it was far easier for me to speak English and gesture, and then wait for a struggled response, than it was to fumble around to draw up what Spanish I could recollect. Basically, I prioritized my own comfort over theirs. I had not created a welcoming environment. I had not been hospitable.

Eventually this realization hit me like a ton of bricks. How could I consider myself a welcoming and hospitable person when I had valued my own comfort over someone else's?

The thought of speaking Spanish after all these years absolutely terrified me. Nonetheless, at the next opportunity, I attempted my rusty Spanish skills, and judging by the looks they gave me, I suspect they might have actually preferred that I go back to speaking in English with exaggerated gestures. But I am working to welcome, to create space into which others can step comfortably, and one of the ways that can we do this is by putting aside our own embarrassment and discomfort so that another person might feel a little less of his or her own.

Catholic priest and spiritual writer Henri J.M. Nouwen wrote about hospitality as a means by which we break through our own fears into a sense of openness. In *Ministry and Spirituality*, he wrote, "Hospitality is the virtue which allows us to break through the narrowness of our own fears and to open our houses to the stranger, with the intuition that salvation comes to us in the form of a tired traveler. Hospitality makes anxious disciples into powerful witnesses, makes suspicious owners into generous givers, and makes close-minded sectarians into interested recipients of new ideas and insights."[19]

Later, in *Reaching Out: The Three Movements of the Spiritual Life*, Nouwen wrote that hospitality is the "creation of free space where the stranger can enter and become a friend instead of an enemy."[20] The purpose of hospitality, he said, "is not to change people, but to offer them space where change can take place. It is not to bring men and women over to our side, but to offer freedom not disturbed by dividing lines."[21]

If we are to believe in an inclusive and universally welcoming God (or if we are to believe in the commonality of the human condition), how can we *not* practice universal hospitality? How can we live a life that is not defined by a constant openness of heart and mind? The truth is we cannot; welcome-ness cannot exist without openness, and hospitality cannot exist without love for the stranger.

All too often, I am finding that we are confusing hospitality with entertaining. Hospitality does not consist of perfectly planned menus and coordinated place settings, nor does it consist of projecting ourselves and our ideals onto others. Hospitality at its sacred core is creating an environment into which friends, enemies, and strangers can enter as if there were no threshold to begin with, a free and clear openness that offers an escape from the world's burdens for a period of time. Hospitality isn't just an open door; it's a hand stretched out the door to welcome others in.

---

[19] Henri J.M. Nouwen, "The Wounded Healer" from *Images of Pastoral Care: Classic Readings*, ed. by Robert C. Dykstra, (Atlanta: Chalice Press, 2005), 81.
[20] Nouwen, *Reaching Out: The Three Movements of the Spiritual Life*, (New York: Doubleday, 1975), 71.
[21] Nouwen, *Reaching Out*, 71.

Matt and I both still enjoy entertaining, and it seems we always have some kind of get-together or dinner party on the horizon. But these days the focus is more about inclusivity, openness, generosity of spirit, and less about matching place settings and guest lists. We offer casual meals with time for conversation instead of carefully planned menus that leave us both tied to the kitchen. Plastic cups and spilled milk. Juice bags and sippy cups. Coats thrown over couches and relaxed smiles.

Hospitality, I'm learning, isn't a dinner party or an event. It's a behavior that thrives in our homes so it can extend beyond those walls and be carried forward into the world. Hospitality is not about perfection or Pinterest-worthy tablescapes; hospitality is about a sloppy and imperfect love for guests and strangers alike.

Grace, after all, is an action, and true grace isn't always easy. Grace—and hospitality as a footprint of grace—cannot just be welcoming those who are like us, and doing what is comfortable and making things look pretty. That isn't grace or hospitality; that's more like a cabaret show or a club with secret handshakes. Grace is about accepting people for who they are, where they are, and as they are. And hospitality is about welcoming people regardless of who they are, where they are, or how they are. Because if we only welcome those who are like us, if we only focus on the "show," we will only ever connect with what's already inside our tightly packed boxes. And, of course, that isn't really connecting with anything at all.

The Spirituality Girls

"Everybody is a story. When I was a child, people sat around kitchen tables and told their stories. We don't do that so much anymore. Sitting around the table telling stories is not just a way of passing time. It is the way the wisdom gets passed along. The stuff that helps us to live a life worth remembering."

—Rachel Naomi Remen

"There's something we need to discuss," Elizabeth began, stopping to look at each of us around her dining-room table.

Oh, no, I thought. *What could she possibly want to discuss? Is something wrong?*

As a group, the five of us had been meeting for the past six years after joining a "small group" at Second Unitarian Church in Chicago. Throughout the years, the exact size and make-up of the group had changed, but for the most part, the five of us had continued to meet on a somewhat regular basis to discuss any number of spiritual topics.

"We need to talk about whether we want to continue meeting and, if so, what direction we want the group to take, how often we should meet, that kind of thing," Elizabeth said.

I felt a shudder move through my legs, my heart raced, and my palms started to sweat. *What will I do if the others don't want to continue meeting? This group is my lifeline right now, the only real spiritual community that I have.* I had stepped away from the group for several months when we first moved to the suburbs, and I had missed the group more than I imagined I would. I had thought that I would simply find a new small group and a new spiritual home easily with the snap of my fingers, but both tasks had proved more difficult than anticipated. And it was because of this renewed appreciation for our group's unique characteristics and its special bond that I was all the more fearful of losing it.

Rachel, a woman who works in theater, adjusted her trendy eyeglass frames on her nose, gently moved her hair off her eyebrow, and confidently said, "Yes. I'd like to continue meeting."

Almost instantly, my pounding heart slowed, the feeling returned to my legs, and I wiped my palms on my jeans. *Thank God, I'm not alone.*

"I need this group," Rachel continued. "Since I haven't found a church home, you all create accountability for me."

She went on to talk about how she felt accountable to the group for her actions, her way of life, and her spiritual path. She explained that when she sensed she was drifting off course from the life she wanted to lead and drifting away from the person she wanted to be, our group allowed her to account for these decisions in a nonjudgmental way.

We simply listened. The group understood that we were all striving for the same thing: to reach our greatest and highest potential as human beings. In that common goal, we provided unwavering support, advice, and guidance to each other.

As I cautiously looked at the others seated around the table—all of us from different religious backgrounds and lifestyles—I noticed we were all subtly nodding our agreement. After Rachel finished talking, we all repeated her sentiments.

I hadn't realized it at the time, but what our little group— the Spirituality Girls, as we call ourselves—amounts to is a church. Within the comforting confines of a safe haven for discussion, we explore our own ideas about how we can live the best life possible and leave a positive imprint on the world, and we challenge each other to do the same. In this way, our small group is a progressive religious movement in and of itself. We are a congregation. We are church.

One does not need to look far to see all the damage that religion and religious differences can cause. The media are awash with news of violence, anger, judgment, and discrimination stemming from religious disagreements. We have become so focused on our own religion, our own spirituality, and our own faith that we have forgotten how to show respectful acknowledgement for other faiths. We have forgotten to consider the importance of another's religion to their culture. We have forgotten to practice those all-important acts of empathy and compassion. And interfaith relations have suffered as a result. God and the Spirit and love are smothered by a cloud of defensiveness, self-importance, and misunderstandings.

All too often, religion forgets the grace part, it forgets the faith part, and it forgets the sharing part.

When we think about spiritual practices, things like prayer, introspection, meditation, and worship come to mind. And while these activities are crucial components of spirituality, they tend to focus on internal behaviors or activities conducted in the company of like-minded individuals. Unfortunately, these activities often lack the recognition that we are a part of this larger web of connection that binds us all together in our shared humanity—that we are a part of a community despite all the inherent cultural and religious differences. By engaging in the intentional practice of faith sharing, however, we can shed our ignorance and connect with humanity on a deeper and more respectful level. Faith sharing as a spiritual practice is God in action, grace in linguistic form.

Faith sharing comes in many varieties, but one of the most obvious forms of faith sharing is good old-fashioned conversation. For instance, the Spirituality Girls and I rarely see each other outside of our monthly get-togethers, but I consider these women to be among some of my dearest friends. We come from different faith backgrounds, different demographics, and different parts of the metro Chicago area, yet we always have one thing in common: our mutual interest in facilitating each other's spiritual accountability by engaging in respectful faith sharing.

We eat. We drink. We talk. We share.

We talk about food, wine, sex, and God. We talk about our jobs, our kids, and our spouses. We reveal our insecurities and concerns, as well as our hopes and dreams. We share our ideas about what it means to live a life of compassion, generosity, justice, and spirituality. We discuss spiritually focused books like Karen Armstrong's *Twelve Steps to a Compassionate Life* or *Zealot* by Reza Aslan. We share our life stories and our faith stories. We offer personal opinions that move beyond pleasantries, small talk, and surface conversation so we can get to what really matters: the Spirit of it all, the Spirit *in* it all.

And in doing so, we share the deepest parts of ourselves. We share our faith, and we share our doubts about God. We share our most vulnerable and sensitive beliefs, laying ourselves raw and fully open to the possibility of knowing each other on a deeper level.

In talking about our beliefs and sharing our faith with each other, we have granted one another a rare glimpse into the deepest recesses of our souls—a place that many of us don't even let our closest friends and family members see.

We live in a society that shuns faith sharing, particularly interfaith communication. We are scared of it. We are afraid of being judged, and we are afraid of judging. We worry that if we talk about sensitive and personal issues, such as faith and spirituality, that we might be forced to acknowledge the differences between us. Many of us religious liberals avoid faith sharing for fear that we might offend someone or because (*gasp!*) we may have to admit that we don't necessarily have a clear understanding of our own faith and beliefs.

Our society doesn't talk about faith, except with those we are fairly certain share our views. We don't ask about the spiritual practices or faith of others unless we want to reinforce our preconceived ideas. We don't share our spiritual beliefs, and we don't want others to share theirs. We keep quiet.

And interfaith relations suffer as a result. We forget that differences do not need to divide us; rather, acknowledging differences can be a means of expanding our options and opening our minds. When we talk about beliefs—not necessarily *what* we believe but *why* we believe—we grant ourselves the opportunity to know someone on a deeper level and open our minds to alternative perspectives. When we share our faith—not just how we practice our faith but how our faith shapes our life—we give someone else the gift of knowing us more intimately.

When we find ourselves shying away from conversations about spirituality and neglect to learn about the faith of others, perhaps we should ask ourselves, *Am I uncomfortable because I am afraid that I will be judged? Or am I uncomfortable because I am unsure of what I believe?*

Certainly, in some cases, the fear of judgment is a very real thing, but ignorance can be exacerbated when we fall prey to the fear of judgment. Other times, we shy away from conversations about our faith simply because we are unsure of what we believe. We have doubts and questions. We see inconsistencies, and there are times when we just don't know what we believe. But there is no shame in admitting the presence of spiritual doubts. In fact, acknowledging doubts is a critical part of an authentic faith.

For many of us, our faith (or maybe lack of faith) is a large part of who we are and how we live our lives. By refraining from talking about our faith, we are preventing ourselves from really getting to know others—both those of different cultures and backgrounds, as well as those people who are closest to us. And when we fail to know and understand others and ourselves, we breed ignorance and judgment. We dehumanize others by diminishing their culture and their faith. We neglect the importance of spiritual community, whether to ourselves or to others. And ultimately we prevent ourselves from opening boxes and creating sacred connection. We keep ourselves from knowing God and sharing the Spirit.

Faith sharing is *not* about proselytizing with the goal of conversion. It doesn't include "should's" or punishments or blame. Faith sharing is about talking and listening and connecting. It is about humanizing other faiths to foster acceptance, respect, and empathy. It is about interfaith education so we can more deeply connect to our own faith while learning about others' faith. It is about respecting the importance of spiritual community to our overall well-being, about honoring the worth of other spiritual communities, about fostering humility and compassion. Above all, faith sharing is about grace.

Religion, for me, isn't about church attendance, rituals, and following rules. It's also not about bullying others to believe what we believe, nor is it about shame and judgment. Religion, for me, is about spiritual community, faith sharing, and grace. It's about opening boxes and tying threads. Religion is about creating sacred connection.

We are social animals. We gather, we assemble, we congregate. We learn in classrooms, we work with colleagues, we live with families, we socialize with friends, and we worship in churches with other parishioners. As Rebecca Parker says, "The question is not *whether* we are social, connected beings. That is a given. The question is *how* we shape our modes of being with one another and with the sources that uphold and sustain life."[22]

Religious community facilitates grace through accountability—not necessarily divine accountability, but personal, social, civic, and moral accountability. Groundbreaking studies revealed in the book *American Grace: How Religion Divides and Unites*

---

[22] John A. Buehrens and Rebecca Ann Parker, *A House for Hope*, (Boston, MA: Beacon Press, 2010), 34.

Us show that religious Americans are generally nicer, happier, and better citizens. Religious Americans tend to be more generous with their time, talent, and resources to both religious and secular causes. They are more likely to join volunteer associations, attend public meetings, and respond more compassionately when others wrong them. But, perhaps, the most startling revelation in the book comes from studies showing that good neighborliness and happiness are attributed not to theology, but rather to religious *communities*. According to the book's authors, "Communities of faith seem more important than faith itself."[23]

Certainly some religions do prioritize rituals, rules, and judgment. Like all institutions, organized religion suffers from its fair share of faults. Even the influential Unitarian minister William Ellery Channing was highly skeptical of organized religions. A prominent leader in the transcendental movement, he advocated for a faith in God that began by looking within ourselves:

> *I call that mind free which jealously guards its intellectual rights and powers, which calls no man master, which does not content itself with a passive or hereditary faith, which opens itself to light [whenever] it may come, which receives new truth as an angel from heaven, which, while consulting others, inquires still more of the oracle within itself.*[24]

Truthfully, I have been repeatedly let down by organized religion. These disappointments have been both minor and severe, and they have all threatened to wear down my faith. I have thought I could connect with my spirituality on my own without the

---

[23] Robert D. Putnam and David E. Campbell, *American Grace: How Religion Divides and Unites Us*, (New York: Simon & Schuster, 2010), 444.
[24] William Ellery Channing, 1830 Election Day sermon entitled "Spiritual Freedom," *The Complete Works of W.E. Channing*, (London: Christian Life Publishing Co., 1884), 166.

involvement of a church, and that I could be spiritual but not religious. But what these internal arguments failed to acknowledge is that religious community is a necessity in order for me to connect fully with my spirituality. While this may not be true for everyone, it is my truth: there is no spirituality without religion for me. Religious community allows me to focus on human kindness, social justice, and the needs of others—all against the mystical backdrop of a transcendent power we cannot fully comprehend. In other words, religious community allows me to live out my spirituality, to not just *be* spiritual, but to act in accordance with the Spirit.

Whether it is church, worship, or faith sharing with the Spirituality Girls, at its very essence, spiritual community is about more than the mere belief in Jesus, Allah, Buddha, Muhammad, or what have you. It is not even about a belief in the existence of God, for that matter. Spiritual community is about opening ourselves up to move beyond the *self* and hold ourselves open to the possibility that there is something *more*. Religious community is about the ultimate belief that the Spirit permeates, that grace heals, and that love wins.

An Uphill Battle

"Something opens our wings. Something makes boredom and hurt disappear. Someone fills the cup in front of us: We taste only sacredness."

—Rumi

When I was six, I wanted to be a teacher. When I was seven, I wanted to raise horses in my parents' backyard. When I was twelve, I thought I wanted to be a therapist or a marriage counselor. When I was eighteen, I decided I wanted to be a lawyer. When I was twenty-two, I realized that I most desperately wanted to be a mom.

And now, at the age of thirty-seven, here I am a writer. In many ways, I think this job of "writer" is like combining all of those previous career plans into one. Well, except for the horse-raising thing.

Or perhaps writing is even more like raising horses than teaching, counseling, or advocating. In fact, it might be a bit like taming wild horses. All of these wild and excitable thoughts race around in my head, but they need to be corralled and tamed, brought together so they make sense and don't go trampling people and breaking down fences.

Writing, for some people I would imagine, is quick-paced and invigorating, an exercise in creativity and imagination. For me, writing is choppy and difficult and always a little wobbly. Wild horses of ideas and fragments of sentences will run through my head at the most inopportune time, such as when I'm jogging on the treadmill, waiting for my car to move through the car wash, or watching Teddy's gymnastics class. Like a wild stallion, these thoughts glide through my head with grace and power. And then when I try to tame them onto the page, they look wild-eyed and panicky and weak.

I am both a writer by trade and a writer by calling and, while both roles involve the act of writing, they are very different. Professionally, I use my legal background and training as an attorney to write marketing materials such as web copy, press releases, newsletters, and the like for attorneys and law firms. As far as jobs go, freelance legal writing is fairly satisfying. The pay is decent, the hours are flexible, and I can go to work in sweatpants and a baseball hat. But it is not a calling in the way that being a mother, writing this book, or leading worship at my church have been a calling.

The calling to write, personally and from the heart, came slowly in whispers of "could I?" and "I don't know" and "maybe…" It came in can't-sleep-at-night stories running through my head. It came in it'll-never-happen cries on Matt's shoulder and in keep-it-up voices of encouragement.

Just because writing has been a calling for me, that doesn't mean it's been easy. In fact, it just might be one of the hardest things I've ever done. I wrote much of this book while reading Brenda Miller and Holly Hughes's book *Pen and Bell*. "I can, I can," they tell me of this writing process.[25] And yet for all their encouragement and advice, so many times I have wanted to scream back, "I can't! I can't!"

Writing, for all the joy that it brings me, is a constant struggle. First, there is the struggle to find the time to write. As a work-at-home mom, there never seems to be enough hours in the day to get the kids to school, throw in a few loads of laundry, walk the dogs, unload the dishwasher, finish a few work projects, help

---

[25] Brenda Miller and Holly J. Hughes, preface to *The Pen and Bell: Mindful Writing in a Busy World*, (Boston: Skinner House, 2012), xvii.

Jackson with his homework, take Teddy to swimming lessons, answer a few work e-mails, and tuck the kids into bed at night. Much less find the time to write a book and submit articles to various publications, and post on my blog or keep up with social media.

Then there are the struggles to create sentences, paragraphs, and chapters that flow and move and come to life, and aren't just a puddle of words splashed on the page. Some of my best writing happens in the shower, waiting outside of Teddy's gymnastics class, in the car at a red light, or in the middle of the night when the clock glows red next to my head. Epiphanies, I tell you, epiphanies. But when I go to write them down, the thoughts come out more like a bad translation of something that could maybe, at one point, have been poetic and prophetic but now just sounds choppy and sophomoric.

And there are the internal struggles to tap into the *guts* of what I really want to say and to fight all the demons of self-doubt that come along with authentic writing. Almost everything worth writing comes with its fair share of questions and doubts: *Can I really say this? What will people think if I write that? Am I being authentic enough? Or is it too honest? Too harsh? Too sappy?* And perhaps the biggest question of all: *Does this speak truth yet still protect the privacy of the other people involved?*

Each article, each chapter, each paragraph, and each sentence is hard earned and comes with a price. Because, as they say, writing is easy—you just open the vein and bleed on paper. The price of satisfying this calling to write is high, paid in blood, sweat, and tears, but the rewards far exceed any price. That's the way it is with a calling, I suppose. The price of *not* doing it is so much higher than any sacrifices or struggles it takes to get there.

With each year of life, it becomes clearer to me that anything that has a measure of purpose and a note of significance involves a certain amount of struggle. The buds of spring struggle to withstand the cold March winds to give us the first pops of color we are so desperate for in April. The friendships and familial relationships we struggle to maintain due to geographical distances, time constraints, and personality differences provide us with the greatest sense of joy and connection. The dark days when we struggle with our own self-doubt and insecurities have the potential to provide us with enhanced clarity and renewed vision.

There are big struggles and small struggles, daily struggles and once-in-a-lifetime struggles, personal struggles and collective struggles. This afternoon I am struggling to put words to the page, to quiet my mind, to focus. It is Sunday afternoon. Matt is catching up on work, and the boys are out with their grandma and grandpa for a much-anticipated visit to the pet store. One dog—Jobe, the anxious one—is sleeping at my feet while the other dog—Maeby, the spunky one—lies regally in a chair across the room. Since it is Sunday, the day of my self-prescribed technology *Shabbos*, the computer is off, my iPhone sits quiet, and I write in pen—an act that I find to be a struggle. As a product and proponent of the technological age, the feel of the pen in my hand is foreign and uncomfortable. I constantly fight the urge to turn the computer on, to check my e-mail or Facebook *just once*. And yet I can already sense that this clumsy pen and the jittery avoidance of distraction has created a kind of quiet focus and contemplative vision that I don't often get when the keys are tapped effortlessly, or there are various websites just waiting to distract me whenever the writing takes me into unfamiliar or vulnerable territory.

When it comes to struggle, there are two things I know to be true. First, struggle is unavoidable, and, second, struggle leads to beauty, purpose, and meaning. And yet, while I know these things with absolute certainty, while I feel the truth of this in my bones, I am habitually praying to avoid struggle, and doing whatever I can to minimize struggle for my family and myself. Of course, part of this is human nature. None of us wants struggle for ourselves or for our loved ones. The entrepreneur doesn't start a business with the hope that the first few years will be so financially challenging that he will eat ramen noodles five nights a week; he hopes to start a business that is an overnight success. A young couple about to start a family doesn't hope to endure years of infertility and a couple of miscarriages to create a family; they hope that the stick has two pink lines shortly after the birth control is tossed in the garbage. The artist doesn't hope to get hundreds of gallery rejections; she hopes to be offered her own show and get discovered.

We hope to get the call and answer it, with an ease that reinforces the notion that *this* is something we are called to do in the first place, that *this* is right, and that *this* is what we are meant to do.

No one wants or asks for struggle, and I don't think that we necessarily should, but why do we hide from it like a dangerous intruder instead of greeting it like an uninvited guest?

Much of our aversion to struggle comes from a lack of faith. A lack of faith that this is our calling, that this is purposeful and has some kind of lasting meaning. We don't think we have the strength to endure the discomfort and pain of struggle. We doubt that the struggle will ever come to pass. We forget that we are not alone, that we are all, in our shared humanity, struggling in some way.

I was talking to a friend last week who was struggling with the decision to have a third child or not. She had already suffered three miscarriages and was unsure whether to continue the struggle to conceive.

"I always thought I would have a big family, that it was my purpose in life," she said. "I want to do something meaningful and worthwhile, but what? I suppose only a handful of people actually change the world. I'm probably just not one of them."

"I guess it all depends on your definition of what it means to change the world," I replied. "If 'changing the world' means finding a cure for cancer and ending apartheid and leading nationwide protests, then I suppose only a handful of people do actually change the world. But me? I think we *all* change the world."

We change the world by raising kind, gentle, and confident children. We change the world by bringing in homeless dogs and cats. By befriending the snot-nosed kid who sits in the back of class and smells a little like onions. By writing and painting and taking pictures. By laughing and hugging and listening. We change the world by writing letters to loved ones *just because*. By saying "thank you" and by holding hands more often than we need to. By struggling to find our calling and then struggling to fulfill that calling. The great civil rights leader Howard Thurman said, "Don't ask what the world needs. Ask what makes you come alive, and go do it. Because what the world needs is people who have come alive."

We change the world by coming alive. And by struggling to come alive.

A few months ago, Matt and I had the good fortune of taking a combined business/leisure trip to Italy. Toward the end of our travels, we spent a couple of days in Cinque Terre, a rugged portion of the Italian Riviera that rests along the Ligurian Sea. Like most tourists in the area, we hiked the trails between the "Five Lands"—the five coastal villages that make up the Cinque Terre. The first leg of the journey is the trail from Monterosso to Vernazza, which is generally thought to be the most difficult portion to traverse. The hills are steep, the paths narrow, the shade sparse, and the sun hot. It is the kind of uphill climb where you just need to put your head down and soldier on.

At one point, while marching up a particularly steep stretch of rocky terrain with head down, sweat dripping in my eyes, my T-shirt soaked completely through, I stopped to let another hiker pass me. I paused, stepped aside, and looked up. The hiker behind me did the same, but he didn't pass.

"Oh, wow. Just *wow*," he breathed with amusement. "I had been concentrating so hard on making it up this hill that I hadn't even noticed just how beautiful it is."

I nodded, partly because I was too out of breath to speak, and partly because I was at a loss for words as well. Diamonds of sunlight danced on the sparkling blue Mediterranean waters, outlined by unforgivingly steep cliffs. To the left, Monterrosso, the town where we'd started this journey, sat nestled into the lush mountainside; on our right, Vernazza, the village where we were headed, seemed to be a million painful steps away. From where we stood, we could clearly see where we had come from and where we were going, not to mention the impressive brilliance that surrounded us *right where we were.*

It can be easy to get consumed with the uphill battle, putting our head down and soldiering on, but sometimes we need to stop and just enjoy the view. Sometimes we need to pause, if only for a moment to catch our breath and marvel at where we've come from, and consider where we are called to go.

In his memoir *On Writing*, Stephen King said, "The scariest moment is always just before you start. After that, things can only get better."[26] And while I agree whole-heartedly that the scariest moment is just before you start (definitely when it comes to writing, but also with most things in life), the most exhausting, grueling, doubt-inducing, soul-crushing, and utterly painful part is the climb—the uphill battle. Things don't always get better after we start. Sure, they might be a little less scary and a little more empowering, but they are not necessarily better.

The fact that things might not be better, or that they might be harder *after* we get started shouldn't make our calling any less purposeful, worthy, or urgent. It is during the middle part, when

---

[26] Stephen King, *On Writing: A Memoir of the Craft*, (New York: Scribner, 2000), 269.

we are beaten and exhausted and filled with doubt, that things most assuredly don't seem "better." When we are in the middle of a tough stretch at work, burning the midnight oil for weeks on end to get the job done. When we have been getting up in the middle of the night for months with a newborn baby. When we are in the dredges of book edits that seem never-ending. It is during these I-don't think-I-can-go-on times that it becomes all the more important to pause when we can, lift up our heads, and take in the view.

The only thing—the absolutely *only* thing—that I have found that makes things "better" after we get over the initial heart-stopping fear of starting is whether or not we open ourselves up a little, let out some of the sorrow and angst, and tether together whatever hope, reassurance, and beauty we can find.

The Comparison Game

"Strive not to be a success, but rather to be of value."
—Albert Einstein

There is this little game I play in my head. It's called the Comparison Game. The rules are simple: look to the outside world for standards and measures of what it means to be successful and worthy, and then deem yourself inferior to that standard. Given that I've been playing this Comparison Game my whole life, I would say I'm pretty good at it. In fact, if there were an Olympic category for the Comparison Game, I would be standing on that podium with the National Anthem playing in the background.

Yes, I think I have mastered the Comparison Game quite well. Honestly, I can't tell you how much time I have spent comparing myself harshly and negatively to, well, just about everyone. To the mom who only feeds her kids healthy, home-cooked, organic meals; the dad who plays tag with his kids at the park while I sit on the bench and scroll through Facebook; the writer with the best-selling book on the store shelves; the mom who proudly sports a pre-baby body just days after giving birth; the neighbor with the beautiful house and well-manicured lawn; the popular friend who hosts the best parties; the acquaintance with the designer clothes and fancy purse; the friend from church who volunteers twenty hours a week; the mom who *never* yells; the friend who *never* loses her cool; the woman at the gym with toned biceps and a flat stomach; the law-school colleague with the high-profile job. . . just to name a few.

But since the Comparison Game isn't an Olympic sport, there are no medals, no fancy prizes, and no free trips to Aruba.

The only thing the Comparison Game has ever given me is a nagging sense of lacking and a separation from joy and what is real and true. Like any sport, the Comparison Game can lead to injury and illness. In this case, it's the disease of dis-ease that thrives on the comparisons and never-enoughs and gotta-haves. It's the side effect of the pursuit of perfection and the quest to "have it all" (as if such a thing existed).

Some of us, I think, are more easily drawn to the Comparison Game than others. Maybe it's because of our harsh inner critic, or because we're scared, or because our skin is a little more permeable than others. Maybe it's because we have an overflowing heart, or we just have a harder time separating ourselves from the cruelty and beauty of the world. Maybe it's because we've got all these Big Questions about purpose, happiness, and success, and these Big Questions seem too overwhelming for us to answer on our own, so we look to others to show us what those things mean.

Looking to others for inspiration or direction is not always harmful, of course. In fact, there is a great deal we can learn from positive mentors, friends, and teachers. The trouble with the Comparison Game is that all too often, the board gets jumbled and flipped over onto its side, and the game pieces are all thrown together into one big mess of perfection. Or, rather, perceived perfection. Instead of success looking like a specific goal, it takes on the shape and form of multiple personas for which there is no way we could ever measure up. In my case, success and happiness looks a lot like a wrinkle-free, tall, thin, best-selling author turned community activist who never yells at her kids, has loads of friends, travels to exotic locations, and never snaps at her husband.

In comparison to this fictional modern-day Barbie, I am undoubtedly a fumbling failure. My career is filled with almost's and close calls. I can't make it more than a couple of days without yelling at my kids, often times with cuss words muttered under my breath but loud enough to hear. I can barely run a couple miles at a modest pace. I have been asked on more than one occasion when my baby is due when I was not pregnant. My laugh lines outline acne and blackheads, and as much as I am madly in love with my husband, I am shamefully outspoken and dramatic, often displacing my stress and frustrations on him.

And something tells me that it's not just me who plays this game and suffers its side effects because I know too many people—men and women, moms and dads, parents of young kids and parents of grown kids—who feel frazzled, exhausted, and perpetually behind. I know too many people who don't have enough time to keep in touch with old friends and family members because of the pressure to do more and have more. I know too many people who feel like they aren't pretty enough or rich enough or thin enough or popular enough or *whatever* enough. I know too many people who struggle mightily to be a good employee, an attentive parent, an affectionate spouse, a well-liked friend, and still find the time to volunteer, exercise, read, go to church, take care of aging parents or sick family members, and (heaven forbid!) get a manicure every once in awhile, because, let's be honest, doing everything and "having it all" is just not possible even if we tell ourselves that it could be if we just tried harder.

In *The Soul of Money*, Lynne Twist writes of this pervasive attitude of "lacking" in our society:

> *For me, and for many of us, our first waking thought of the day is "I didn't get enough sleep." The next one is "I don't have enough time." Whether true or not, that thought of* not enough *occurs to us automatically before we even think to question or examine it . . . Before we even sit up in bed, before our feet touch the floor, we're already lacking something. And by the time we go to bed at night, our minds race with a litany of what we didn't get, or didn't get done, that day . . . What begins as a simple expression of*

the hurried life, or even the challenged life, grows into the great justification for an unfulfilled life.[27]

This attitude of scarcity, lacking, and never-enough starts out with not enough time or sleep or something simple like that, and continues throughout the day with a never-ending litany of all the things we are lacking: time, money, beauty, friends, happiness, respect, admiration, strength, patience . . . the list goes on and on. And with each not-enough, we untie any knots of connection that might have been there.

What this is really about is bad math. I've never been particularly good at math (and I'll admit I needed a calculator a few weeks ago to help Jackson with his first-grade math homework), but I know there is something gigantically wrong with the math that goes into the Comparison Game. Because when you add up things like salaries, property values, square footage, numbers on the scale, billable hours, profit margins, and annual sales, and when you use rulers that measure in Facebook friends and Twitter followers and popularity and fitting in, the math never comes out right. Math like this just leaves us scribbling at our tiny little desks, peering over our shoulders at everyone else, convinced that *they* have the answers, that *they* understand the equations, and that *they* know how to make it work. We sit at our desks alone and scared and absolutely convinced that the answer key was passed out the day we were absent. We sit sweaty, desperate, and knowing we have fallen far behind, certain we will fail or that we are already failing.

But in the end there is no Jumbotron flashing the latest stats of the Comparison Game because we are only playing it against ourselves. This class in bad math was never on the syllabus because these numbers don't really count.

---

[27] Lynne Twist, *The Soul of Money: Transforming Your Relationship with Money and Life*, (New York: W.W. Norton and Company, 2003), 44.

Grace counts, kindness counts, and connection counts. Grace is new math. Grace is hugs and smiles multiplied by true friends, and laughter multiplied by hands held, and dreams shared multiplied by forgiveness and tenderness. Sunsets and block parties and dancing in the kitchen. Cuddles and good-night kisses and singing off-key. Cookies baked and meals shared. I-love-you's and I'm-sorry's and I-forgive-you's. Grace is all of these things, added and multiplied to the power of *infinity*. Those are the numbers that count, and that is the math that adds up to a life well lived.

I know too many people who separate, package, and hide. I know too many people who are playing this Comparison Game and suffering from its side effects of inadequacy and a sense of lacking. I know too many people who are using bad math.

At the end of this game of comparisons and measuring, there are no winners, no medal stands, and no trophies. There is only disconnection from the Spirit, from ourselves, from others, from the interdependent web, because the easier it is to compare, measure, and judge ourselves, the easier it is for us to compare, measure, and judge others. Other people become labels and measuring sticks, instead of intricately complex fibers of the web.

As a Unitarian Universalist, I am committed to the truth that there is an inherent worth and dignity in every person, including ourselves. In order to uphold this truth, we cannot fall victim to the comparisons, measurements, and quest for some standard of perceived perfection. To honor the inherent worth and dignity of every person, we must simply get up in the morning, do our best, and love ourselves at the end of the day. We need to quit this grueling Comparison Game and walk out of the class teaching bad math; we are sweaty and browbeaten enough.

But knowing a truth and living a truth are two very different things. And as a reformed perfectionist, each day must be an intentional choice not to use bad math and not to play this brutal and nasty game. Over the years, I have learned that compassion, forgiveness, and authenticity help a lot. So does throwing my hands up and saying, "Good enough!" every now and then, along with heaps and heaps of kindness. It takes a bit of faith and surrender as well—to God, a higher power, luck, or what have you. And I'm absolutely *certain* that it takes vulnerability and courage and surrounding myself with people who love me, wholly and unconditionally.

The Comparison Game might be one of the only games in which the quitters actually win. But do they ever win big! The prize for quitting the Comparison Game and breaking our pencils over this bad math is nothing short of self-acceptance, happiness, sacred connection, and knowledge of what is real and true.

The prize is grace and joy, open boxes, and woven threads.

The Real Story

"Life is cruel. Yet I have found that there is a grief that is
infused with the grace of God."
—Marianne Williamson

One night a few months ago, instead of picking out a book
before bed, Jackson picked up a photo album and announced that
looking through these old photos would be our story for the night.
The album he chose consisted entirely of photos taken during the
months leading up to his birth and the first six months of his life. It
was filled with the typical baby photos—pictures of an expectant
mom proudly displaying a new crib, a wrinkly newborn, a round-
faced three-month-old flashing his first smiles, a five-month-old on
the beach.

We lay on the floor, stomachs pressed into the carpet and
our shoulders touching. He turned the pages slowly, soaking it all
in with a mixture of fascinated interest and uncomprehending
detachment. He asked questions from time to time: "Is that me?"
"Where is Teddy?" "Was this my room when we lived in Chicago?"
"Was that Grandpa Beach?" But for the most part, he just looked
at the photos, recreating the story of pregnancy, birth, and infancy
in his mind.

As he flipped the pages of the photo album, a nervous
anxiety pulsated through my body. *Will he look at those photos and
discover the truth? Will he see it written on my face? Will he see it in my eyes?
Will the beads of sweat on my forehead now and my shaking hands and voice
give away my secret?*

After a few more questions and several turns of the pages,
we reached the end of the photo book. As I slid it back into its

spot on the shelf along with the other stories of family memories, I let out a deep breath, relieved that Jackson was able to see the story that a baby album should tell—a story of expectation, love, hope, innocence, and tenderness.

But that story is a story of half-truths; there is another story—the *real* story—hidden inside this typical story of baby love.

And if you were to look very closely, you might catch glimpses of this hidden, darker story. Because amidst the photos of a mother and son napping on the couch and new parents cuddling their newborn is a secret I tried for years to bury. It's the real story of a woman desperately lost, struggling to love her baby, and sinking dangerously close to rock bottom.

Looking back, with some distance and increased self-awareness, I see that the cloud of post-partum depression descended shortly after my son was born even though I didn't realize it at the time. Everything—from nursing to sleeping and even cuddling—felt lifeless and horribly wrong. Each day felt like a wave had washed over me and I was drowning, gasping for air, and flailing my arms to stay afloat. I felt detached and disconnected from this new role as mom. *Wait a minute,* I wanted to scream. *I am supposed to love and nurture and feed and clothe and diaper and soothe this little human being with no sleep? I can't do it!* I felt angry and resentful toward this tiny, innocent, and completely vulnerable person. I sunk into some kind of desperate black hole, where all I could see were the things he was taking from me—sleep, independence, my boobs, and control over my bladder. I couldn't see all the things he was bringing into our lives.

Most days I wandered absent-mindedly from room to room, wondering what to do with him and what to do with myself. I busied myself with thank-you notes and Snapfish photo albums and cookies. Lots and lots of cookies. I moved through the day with an energized mixture of caffeine, sugar, and fear. I called my husband at work a lot. I cried a lot. I stared into space and thought about all my friends who were going to Happy Hours, sleeping in on Saturday mornings, and going for a walk around the block without peeing themselves. And I kind of hated each of them just a little bit for it.

A tiny part of me hated Matt for escaping this lonely and bitter existence each day when he left for work. And in some dark corners of my heart, I might have even hated this baby just a little for making my life so difficult and unmanageable and unpredictable. Of course, I didn't really hate my husband or baby; these feelings were really just hiding the deep hatred that I felt for myself and the all-consuming guilt that I felt for having these horrible, selfish, heartless, and shameful thoughts.

Where is the love and affection and connection I'm supposed to be feeling? Why is this all so hard? Why am I not happier given that this life as a stay-at-home-mom is what I've always wanted? And why am I thinking such horrible, shameful thoughts?

Depression, confusion, loneliness, guilt, and shame all muddled together, swirling and expanding to create the perfect emotional storm, a hurricane of sorts. I got pretty good at pretending, though. I played the role of proud new mom, denied that I had a problem, and told everyone I was happy because I knew I *should* be happy. Only I most definitely was not.

Hints of the real story are scattered throughout these photos, however. You can see it in the haunted eyes that stare back at the camera on Christmas morning, in the stilted half-smiles that took all my energy to muster, and in the gloomy slouch of my shoulders. You can see it in the worried look flickering across my husband's eyes in a few of the photos. The real story of post-partum depression is not a solitary story and I wasn't the only one to suffer. In some ways, Matt was suffering with his own post-partum depression by proxy, I suppose. Sleep-deprived and exhausted, fearful of his wife's unpredictable and volatile moods, confused about what to do and how to help, and overwhelmed with his new role as "sole financial provider," the real story is that my husband was taken hostage by this disease too.

Fortunately, the real story is also one of recovery and resilience. Slowly, over a long period of time in a two-steps-forward-one-step-back kind of way, I began to feel less like I was drowning and more like I was treading water until, eventually, I actually felt like I might be swimming. Sure, some days felt like swimming upstream, but I was swimming nonetheless. And if you look closely at those photos, you might be able to see this part of the real story when the darkness began to fade from my eyes, the smiles rendered easier and less forced, and my body stood more straight and sure.

No photo album could ever communicate the epilogue of the real story either. Just like the photos don't show the extent of the desperation and sadness, no photo could ever capture the intense and downright fierce mama love I feel for my son. There is an almost illogical protective bond between us, like a deep and jagged battle scar. No photo could ever capture the gratitude and appreciation I have for my husband, for his patience, support, and ability to always tell it like it is, and then to love me enough to bring me back to life. No photo could contain the relief I felt when my second son was born three years later and, by the grace of God, we were spared the dark hurricane this time around.

No photo is able to capture the shame and regret I still feel today. The camera doesn't see the tiny and oh-so-sharp knife that pierces my heart when I am around new parents, and photos don't show the vice grip clutching my soul whenever I hold a baby, reminding me of all the ways I wish my experience had been different. The photos don't capture the part where shame and regret lingered even though the sadness, loneliness, and desperation are long gone. My head knows I didn't choose post-partum depression, but I wonder if part of me—the heart part—won't always feel like it was a character flaw, like I failed my son and my husband, like I was a less capable mom, and like I was robbed of something that every parent deserves—contentment and peace.

It would be easier, I suppose (and certainly more pleasant), to adopt the half-truth story, the one that people want to see and the one that I wish were real. But I am learning that by owning and accepting our stories, regardless of how gritty and knotted they might be, we can take the first steps toward getting over the shame and regret. By telling our stories, we can empower others to own, accept, and share their stories as well. It is in that owning and accepting that we infuse these real stories of love and loss, of desperation and forgiveness, of weakness and resilience with the succulent aroma of grace. It is in the telling and sharing of these real stories that we harness that transformative power of sacred connection.

As relieved as I was that night that the photos told the story they were supposed to tell, that Jackson was able to look at them and marvel at his growth and development, I hope that one day when he's grown he will look at the photos and see the real stories within them. Because as much as I hope that he will look at the photos and be reminded of his inherent worth and significance simply by virtue of the fact that he was born and was loved, I pray that one day, many years from now, he will be wise enough, confident enough, and compassionate enough to look at these photos and know that they only tell a half-truth, not the real story. I pray he will be able to understand and hold that story: the story of an intentional and committed love, of desperation and forgiveness, of struggle and triumph, of hard-earned happiness and long-awaited contentment. I pray that he will know the beauty of the real story lies not just in the growth of a baby, but in the growth of a faithful and dedicated *family*.

We've all got our stories. There are the polite small-talk stories we exchange with our work colleagues and parents at school drop-off. There are the sound-bite stories we post to Facebook. There are the made-up stories we sometimes tell ourselves, the half-truth stories we tell family and friends, the stories of omission we communicate with our silence. And then there are the *real* stories—the awkward stories, the painful stories, the complicated stories, and also the beautiful stories. These are the good stories, the grace-filled stories. We are meant to accept and share these stories if we ever have a chance at a sacred connection, because these real stories are so much deeper and richer, so much stronger and more satisfying, than any half-truth story—if for no other reason than the fact that they are *our* stories.

So whatever your real story is—whether it's picture-perfect or dark and blemished—own it and accept it. And when you're ready, tell your story with kindness and tenderness, because inside the gnarled and complicated real story, there is a resilient grace and a quiet power. And with each real story shared comes a tiny slice of freedom and another thread of sacred connection.

Sixth-Grade Gym Class

"While it is important for people to see your promise, you must also remember that hope is the keeper of both happiness and disappointment, the father of both progress and failure."
—Bryant H. McGill

When I received my first rejection as a writer, I cried my eyes out. Actually, it wasn't even a rejection, per se, it was a second-to-last-place finish in a weekly writing competition, but it may as well have been a rejection. It had the same acrid stench and bitter aftertaste of rejection; it was the same lead balloon in my stomach that felt kind of like a cross between the stomach flu and a punch to the gut.

Shortly thereafter I got my first real rejection. "Thank you for your submission," it read, "but we regret to inform you that…"

The rest of the e-mail didn't matter, the end result was the same. I had been told "no," which, naturally, my mind interpreted as "you aren't good enough." Pretty soon, each "no" grew and expanded. It wasn't long before every "no" sounded like "you kind of suck" and "you will never be good enough" and "not only is your work not good enough, but your hair is a little frizzy today and it looks like you've put on a few pounds too."

Over the years, I have received hundreds of rejections. Many of them have been justified; either my submission wasn't my best work or it wasn't right for the publication. Other times the rejections seemed baseless, personal, and almost discriminatory. While I expected some rejections and I was able to sidestep them with nary a stumble, others jumped out at me, knocking me to the ground in a wounded, crumbled mess of tears for days. Regardless of the attention I gave each one and the extent of its impact on me, each "no, thank you" left me with the metallic taste of rejection and a cluttered pile of questions about my worth.

Even those rejections that I accepted piled on top of all the rejections in a heap of dirty negatives, out of which grew weeds of uncertainty that hadn't been there before. Whether it was getting passed up for a job that I didn't really want, losing a spot on the speaking roster, or not getting invited to a wedding that I wouldn't have been able to attend anyway. Even benign rejections that saved me from something (or someone) had a way of magnifying all of the other rejections until a tiny grain of dirt looked like a mountain of trash.

Rejections aren't just about turned-down book proposals, unachieved job promotions, or unreturned phone calls for a second date. The sting of rejection happens when we hear that dreaded word "no." We feel rejection when we are on the outside looking in, when our needs are met with silence, and when we don't feel heard or understood.

In junior high I spent a lot of time in gym class hiding behind lockers and standing against the wall waiting to be picked. Despite the fact that I was a swimmer, I was about the most un-athletic and uncoordinated person in the gym. Almost every day, without fail, I would be one of the only two girls left standing against the gym wall, waiting to be chosen by a team. *Pick me, please pick me,* I would think. *Don't let me be the last person picked. Please, God, don't let me be the last person picked.*

I would push my glasses up my nose, cross my arms in front of my flat chest, and let out a sigh. *Don't cry if they don't pick you. Do. Not. Cry.*

But the tears would be already stinging my corneas, threatening to escape in an emotional avalanche of frustration, insecurity, and sadness.

"We'll take Christie," one of the team captains might finally say, and my heart would leap.

Oh, thank God I'm not last, I would think before realizing I was second to last. Twenty-some other girls had been chosen for a volleyball team before me. Immediately, the tears would spring up again, threatening to release themselves and splatter down the front of my white gym tee.

Rejection. Disappointment. Setback.

Such ugly and loaded words, attaching shadows where before there had been lightness and satisfaction.

Each time I was left standing against the wall as other girls were chosen for teams, I would think, *Why do I care so much? I don't even like volleyball.* In fact, I hated volleyball. I hated the way the ball stung my forearms when I tried to bump (or was it set?) the ball back across the net. I hated the way I never seemed to jump high enough to volley the ball back over the net. I hated the way the ball would spring back from the net every time it was my turn to serve, reminding everyone why I had been chosen last or second to last.

But even though volleyball (or any P.E. sport for that matter) was not my thing, I didn't want to be picked last. I didn't want to feel rejected and inadequate.

It seems these feelings of middle-school gym class never really go away, they just kind of simmer down like lava bubbling in a dormant volcano. They bubble up when we don't get into the college of our choice, or the cute boy in physics class doesn't ask us to prom. They grow to a simmer after our heart is broken for the first time, even if it's broken by a boy we knew wasn't Mr. Right. They boil when we are turned down for job after job, when we are laid off, or when our colleague down the hall gets the job promotion. They smolder up when we see friendships fade away, when we aren't invited to the neighborhood party, or when a gaggle of PTA moms laugh coyly about something and we're certain that they must be laughing at us.

A little while back, I auditioned for a spot in a local production about motherhood during which twelve writers would read their stories to a live audience. The piece I selected was poignant, authentic, and just a little heartbreaking—you know, all those things that define motherhood. I made it through the first round of cuts and was given an opportunity to audition for the show a few weeks later. I was confident in the quality of my piece, but shortly before the audition, I realized I had serious doubts that the piece was appropriate for this type of show. I also looked at the rehearsal schedule and considered the time commitment that would be involved if I were chosen for the show, and realized this was not an opportunity I could take on at this point in my life. I secretly regretted submitting the piece and agreeing to audition.

"I almost hope I don't make it," I confessed to Matt the night before the audition. "I just don't have it in me to commit to something like this right now."

Despite my misgivings, I showed up and put my best foot forward. I read my story, knowing deep in my heart that it was a story that needed to be told. When I received the rejection two days later ("unfortunately . . . not able to cast you . . . nothing personal . . ."), I should have been relieved. I wouldn't have to sacrifice multiple weekends at rehearsals. Instead, I could spend that time relaxing with my family, working on other writing projects, and maybe even taking an afternoon nap. I should have been relieved—*you didn't want this*, I told myself—but really all I felt was disappointment, sadness, and inadequacy.

After I read the e-mail announcing the cast, I was transported back to sixth-grade gym class again, standing against the wall, rejected and left behind, while others were chosen for something I didn't even want to do. I wonder if, as adults, we aren't still the same scared and insecure kids we used to be, just with saggier breasts and bigger thighs and wrinkles where there used to be pimples.

Where does this desperate need for approval come from? Why does the knife of rejection draw so much blood? And, more importantly, how can we respond to rejection with grace so we can use disappointment and setbacks to cultivate connection rather than separation?

Questions of adequacy and worth come into play anytime we care deeply about something, whether it's our family, children, job, friends, or even personal identities. Anytime we devote a significant amount of time and energy to something—knitting, writing, photographing, painting, investment banking, lawyering, teaching, parenting, nursing, building, running, bowling, or what have you—we want positive results and acknowledgement. We want to know that our time, energy, and devotion were worthwhile.

Other times, the need for acceptance is fueled by a competitive drive. Competition can be a useful tool in many respects; it rewards hard work and encourages high-quality efforts, fosters self-awareness of our strengths and weaknesses, and cultivates accountability and responsibility. But when we are competitive with the subjective facets of our lives—personality traits, values and priorities, creative outlets, artistic skills, spiritual growth—competition becomes a barrier to connection.

Disappointments happen. We cannot win every race. We may lose our job or be passed up for the promotion. A lover may leave us, a marriage may end in divorce, or a friendship may dwindle. A proposal we have worked on for weeks may be declined, a competitor might win the business account, or a manuscript we have poured our heart into may be rejected hundreds of times. The fertility treatments might not work, the adoption might fall through, or an adult child might decide to move far away from us.

But rejection and disappointment and setbacks do not need to separate. We do not need to put our hopes and dreams into their separate little boxes, tightly secure the lid, and lock them away. We can hold those hopes and dreams up to the light, and use

101

the frayed threads of rejection and disappointment to tie them together. We can create a banner of hope from our broken hearts, hidden dreams, and desperations.

Anne Lamott wrote in *Plan B: Further Thoughts on Faith:* "Hope is not about proving anything. It's about choosing to believe this one thing, that love is bigger than any grim, bleak shit anyone can throw at us."[28] And that is just one of the many reasons I absolutely adore Saint Anne. Hope is bigger, love is stronger, faith is brighter. Tied together, the banner of hope is absolutely breathtaking.

Each rejection is a gift of sorts, one that may not be opened for many years to come. We need to hear a million no's before we can get to a yes. Because without all those no's, the yes wouldn't really be a yes at all. It would be something more like a shoulder shrug and a "maybe" or a half-hearted "I suppose." And isn't YES what we're really after?

Sometimes disappointment and setback carry a cosmic purpose with them, for each closed door that we meet is an open door for someone else. The job offer we didn't receive was probably given to another candidate, perhaps someone who needed the job more than we did. Someone else might be drinking bubbly and celebrating the prize we didn't win. When we fulfill our divine purpose as a fiber in the interdependent web, which sometimes requires that we be met with a closed door of rejection, we inevitably contribute to the universal whole whether we realize it or not.

Conversely, when we draw into our rejections, closing the lids over ourselves out of embarrassment, anger, or frustration, we inevitably sever a few critical fibers in the web whether we realize it or not, if for no other reason than we have allowed the closed

---

[28] Anne Lamott, *Plan B: Further Thoughts on Faith,* (New York: Penguin Books, Ltd., 2005), 275.

doors to make us feel inferior and unworthy. As Eleanor Roosevelt said, "No one can make you feel inferior without your consent."

Well, I don't know about you, but I am a pushover for that whole inferiority thing; I just can't seem to say "No, thank you" or "Take a hike!" when rejection comes knocking at my door selling bushels full of inferiority, shame, and doubt. Instead, of turning that old bullhead away, I find myself opening the door and saying, "Okay, I guess I'll take whatever it is you're selling." And then once I've got inferiority, shame, and doubt lining my shelves, I might as well start playing the Comparison Game and closing the lids on a few boxes as well.

Not consenting to inferiority, and choosing instead the path of acceptance and acknowledgement, is a tough path to walk. Like most things, I have found that it requires a whole lot of practice, some trial and error, and plenty of self-care.

But I have also found that it gets easier with practice, as well. And when we accept and acknowledge our disappointments, instead of buying the jumbo-size box of inferiority and shame, we create this sliver of space into which others can step from under their own clouds of rejection. With grace and kindness—mostly for ourselves and our shortcomings—we can tear down the fences that divide us and instead reach across the divide in our shared humanity. Because if there is one thing of which I am certain, it is that no one—absolutely *no one*—will get to the end of their life and say, "Wow, now that was easy, I sure wish I had been given a little more rejection and disappointment." No one.

So why not acknowledge rejection and the feelings that it conjures up as just another commonality of the human condition? Why not say at the end of a long day, "Well, that was kind of shitty and I'm hurting a bit right now, can you help me?" Why not say "no thank you" to the feelings of inferiority, shame, and doubt that rejection tries to hustle? We've got a full pantry stocked with love and mercy, second chances and new beginnings, hope and kindness already; we don't need those things that rejection wants to sell.

Why don't we allow grace to string together our doubts and fears with our hopes and dreams, building a banner that sparkles with the light of vulnerability, empathy, and understanding, and sprinkles love, creativity, and kindness?

Now *that* would be something worth buying.

Rose-Colored Glasses

"Could a greater miracle take place than for us to look through each other's eyes for an instant?"
—Henry David Thoreau

Way deep down, in one of the jumbled bins of toys scattered throughout my house, there's a pair of yellow-tinted sunglasses with the words "Happy Birthday" emblazoned across the top. Every once in a while, the kids and I will pull out the sunglasses (never on someone's birthday, of course) and take turns putting them on. The color of the lenses isn't anything dramatic, just a pale yellow hue, but the transformation that takes place once the glasses are slipped on is absolutely remarkable. The ordinary suddenly looks strangely unrecognizable under that phosphorescent glow, and it's hard to imagine what things had looked like without the yellow birthday glasses to filter the view.

The glasses soften and brighten everything, giving the tangible an almost ethereal feel. With the glasses on, the world seems a little less harsh but more ambiguous, warmer but more perplexing. It is *almost* like looking through another person's eyes for the briefest moment. And could there be a more transformative and powerful experience than to see things from inside the heart, mind, and soul of another person?

Tinted glasses must be getting harder and harder to find because it seems like empathy is a vanishing art. Judgment, criticism, blame, and condemnation are brandished about with abandon, sometimes covertly lurking in dark corners and other times wielded wildly like a sword.

Judgment and criticism like to masquerade as advice and opinions, but make no mistake they are very different. Advice and differences of opinion should be welcomed, encouraged, and greeted with an open heart and curious mind. The advice of a trusted friend, guidance from a respected mentor, and the opinions of someone with particular skill or expertise are invaluable, and I will seek them out at every chance. But judgment and criticism? Well, those things just seem to make everyone feel a little icky.

But what would happen if instead of rushing to rash judgments and unfounded criticism we tried to really see and feel things from another person's perspective?

As a parent, I am no stranger to judgment and criticism. After all, I have been disparaged by a little old lady in Old Navy for letting my son carry a giant white teddy bear around the store! I have also been judged by peering eyes at the library while my son runs up and down the aisles screaming. I have been silently judged too many times to count by everyone from family members to teachers to strangers on the street. I have chastised myself with a seemingly endless stream of doubts and second-guesses.

We have judged and we have been judged. I know I have judged others, even on those occasions when I tried my best not to judge. I have criticized in unsolicited advice and passive-aggressive suggestions.

We judge sometimes even without saying a word. But regardless of whether our judgments and criticisms are held in our minds or veiled in "justifications," judgment and criticism hurt not only those we judge and criticize; they hurt our own relationship with God and deter the exhibition of grace.

We cannot know the personal demons another person is wrestling with. We cannot know the true nature of the cards another person has been dealt. We cannot know what it's like see the world through another person's eyes, to know the world from another person's mind, or to feel the world with another person's fingers. But with radical empathy, we just might get a glimpse.

Imagine what our life might look like if instead of judging, we asked the tough questions; if instead of pointing our finger, we examined our own role; if instead of blaming, we listened; if instead of responding in anger, we offered sympathy and understanding.

Imagine what society might look like if we respected *all* love, and examined the nature of our own marriages before we condemned the love of others. Imagine what our workplaces might look like if, instead of blaming seemingly lazy co-workers we considered the possible internal conflicts they may be suffering and offered our assistance. Imagine how our moods might be altered if, instead of dropping F-bombs at the driver who cut us off, we prayed that the driver's distracted mind might be eased. Imagine how our communities might look if, instead of judging the mom who placates her kids with lollipops while shopping in Target or snaps too harshly, we looked her in the eye and said, "I know it's tough. Let me carry your bags to your car."

Imagine what our home life might look like if we overlooked the socks on the floor and the snappy moods and, instead of greeting our partner with admonishments, we welcomed him or her into our arms at the end of the day. Imagine what our families might look like if as we bumped elbows with one another, and we mustered up the courage to really *know* each other, gritty warts and all. Imagine what our relationships might look like if, instead of withdrawing from the ugliness, we sank into it armed with radical empathy.

Imagine what our own souls might look like if we let down our walls, accepted our conflicting emotions, and embraced the messiness of life. Imagine what the world might look like if, instead of looking *at* each other, we looked *within* each other so we could see beyond the neatly packaged exteriors, with our juicy and messy interiors laid bare and exposed.

Criticism and judgment are natural human responses to dealing with what goes on around us. Empathy is more than just sympathy, which is the desire to ease another's pain; rather, empathy is the ability to feel another's pain. Empathy—*radical empathy*—takes *hard work* because it asks that we do more than pity the pitiful, but also that we seek to understand the incomprehensible. And, unfortunately, sometimes we sell ourselves short, believing we're not up to the task. We treat our souls like fragile statues that need to be protected. We secretly fear that our minds are incapable of handling a convoluted, muddled mess of conflicting viewpoints and alternative perspectives. We tell ourselves that our hearts' flexibility is finite, at risk of snapping like a rubber band if stretched too far with all the sorrow, bewilderment, and ecstasy that lie within the collective psyche.

But our souls are strong, so much stronger than we ever thought possible. Our hearts are competent enough to navigate the chaotic maze of ideas and perspectives. Our hearts are infinitely pliable, begging to be stretched to the brink with the full array of human emotion.

The beauty of living in a grace-filled community is that we can count on one another to give us the benefit of the doubt because we will do the same for them. We can count on one another not to judge us by the microcosms of our life to which they are witness, but to understand that there is a plethora of complexities to which no one but God is witness. We can rely on others to celebrate us as children of God who are inherently worthy of celebration. In a grace-filled community, we are all just doing the best we can with the hand we've been dealt. In a grace-filled community, we assume best intentions and we jump into each other's hearts and minds to swim around for a while.

We grant radical empathy.

There's enough poisonous judgment and criticism in this world to kill us a thousand times over. But we have an antidote: empathy. It is grace in mind, spirit, and action. It is God's love manifested in the most challenging but connective way. It's perhaps the greatest gift one person could ever give another. And it

just might be the only thing that ever really mattered. Empathy—
radical empathy—could very well be what saves us.

Or, at a minimum, it might help pry open up some of
those tightly closed boxes.

Overflowing

"The heart that breaks open can contain the
whole universe."
—Joanna Macy

As a child, I felt too much. I was sensitive and brooding, dramatic and temperamental. Hearing about an earthquake on the news could keep me up for nights. Hearing my parents in the midst of an adult squabble about money or in-laws or neighbors was like a kick in the stomach. Losing my favorite Strawberry Shortcake doll was like a death in the family.

I cried often and fiercely. I worried constantly and passionately. I clung to regrets and disagreements and anxieties like a ratty old teddy bear.

"Don't be so sensitive," adults would tell me. "You need a thicker skin."

In kindergarten, I cried so hard sometimes that the teacher would send me to the hall, where I would cry even harder until eventually my mom would be called to come get me.

"She needs to learn not to care so much," my kindergarten teacher told my mom. "She can't be such a perfectionist."

Child psychologists might have labeled me a highly sensitive child; teachers called me a perfectionist; my family probably just thought I was difficult. Whatever the label or the characterization, the only solution I heard was to feel less, care less, and somehow grow a thicker skin. But how does one even *do* that? How does a person just shut off the switch on emotions and feelings, hopes and dreams, fears and concerns?

As I moved through adolescence and adulthood, I tried to care less, rebelling in my own fairly safe ways like dating a boy my parents disliked or smoking a few cigarettes in college. I tried to feel less, playing the role of a confident and self-assured woman, even though inside I was terrified and unsure and always second-guessing. And, believe me, if there were some kind of dietary supplement I could've bought at the local GNC to thicken my skin, I would have done it.

For so many years I tried to care less and feel less and grow that illusive thicker skin, but nothing seemed to work.

And then I made the realization that changed my entire life: I wasn't highly sensitive or a perfectionist or difficult; I just had an overflowing heart. Maybe I didn't need to care less or feel less or grow a thicker skin. Maybe I didn't need to change at all. Maybe I just had to learn how to catch the overflow—the emotions, desires, and passions—and make something beautiful out of it.

Those of us with thin skins and overflowing hearts might be the ones who cry hard and sloppily, but we're also the ones who will hold you and rock you and say "hush now, it'll be okay" when you are crying. We might be the ones who stay up at night wondering why the neighbor snubbed us in the grocery store, but we are also the ones who will listen to a neighbor bemoan her health problems in the cereal aisle. We might be hot-tempered and overly dramatic, but we are also quick to forgive and quick to apologize. We might cry at diaper commercials and cell phone commercials and just about every Apple commercial ever made, but we also hug and kiss and jump up and down. We might care too much about little things that shouldn't matter—petty differences, minor squabbles, and teensy-tiny disappointments—but we also care too much about all the little things that *should* matter: family dinners, laughing until you cry, and hand-written notes from old friends. We might feel too much sadness, fear, and doubt, but we also feel much joy, excitement, and pleasure just to be alive. We might have a thin skin, letting in too much of the nastiness, but that thin skin of ours also lets out compassion, mercy, and hope.

Our skin might be thin, our hearts overflowing, but maybe that isn't so bad. Maybe it's actually a *good* thing. Maybe the overflowing heart isn't something to be afraid of or ashamed of. Maybe the overflowing heart isn't something that should be put down. Maybe the overflowing heart isn't something that should be changed or hardened, but something that just needs a bucket to catch all of the emotion, generosity, and grace that seeps out.

Max Lucado wrote in *Grace*, "Your heart is a Dixie cup, and his grace is the Mediterranean Sea. You simply can't contain it all. So let it bubble over. Spill out. Pour forth . . . When grace happens, generosity happens. Unsqaushable, eye-popping bigheartedness happens."[29]

So I've stopped trying to grow a thick skin, stopped trying to care less or feel less, stopped trying to close the value on my overflowing heart. Instead, I'm letting the Dixie cup of my heart grow and expand and overflow so I can be washed clean, so others might drink from the well of compassion. I'm holding open the valve just a crack so the universe can crawl in, and so what comes out might help me connect more deeply and completely and soulfully with others. I'm paddling around in the overflowing excess because that seems to be where the magic happens. When the valve is open, and the harshness and beauty of this human world is seeping in and pouring out, grace is like a bucket for all the hurt and joy, and the brokenness just doesn't seem to matter so much. When the valve is open and the heart is overflowing, the sacred and human worlds can collide, mixing and swirling together in a rainbow of colors so bright you can't tell where one ends and the other begins.

---

[29] Max Lucado, *Grace*, 110.

So maybe the answer *isn't* to care less or feel less, to grow a thicker skin or put a stopper on the valves of our hearts. Maybe the answer is to live a life that is so overflowing, and so permeable that, when we reach the end, we aren't quite sure where we stop and where the Divine begins.

And so my wish for all the highly sensitive children out there, and all the adults with overflowing hearts, is that we may continue to be filled to overflowing. May we be filled with so much love and hope and courage that it seeps through our pores and rains down on our children and our lovers, neighbors, and friends. May we be filled with just enough heartache, struggle, and pain that our finely tuned spiritual recyclers convert it into empathy, compassion, and kindness.

May we be filled to the point of overflowing, and may we let ourselves be emptied to the point of parched hunger so we can be refilled to overflowing again.

Waiting While I Wait

"For love would be love of the wrong thing; there is yet faith. But the faith and the love and the hope are all in the waiting."

—T. S. Eliot

I have come to think of the winter of 2014 as the "winter that wouldn't end." As I write this, phrases like "polar vortex" and "extreme weather" are parts of everyday conversation. I think this Chicago winter might go down in history as one of the longest, coldest, and snowiest on record.

I've become so tired and weary this winter—this "Winter of Woe," as I heard one local newscaster call it—that I find myself switching the channel during the local news weather segments in the hopes that someone else will have better news. But, of course, they all say the same thing: cold, snowy, and windy.

After three very long months of sub-zero wind chills and mountains of snow, I think many of us are throwing our hands up for mercy. Enough already!

The cold and the snow and the bitter wind, the snow pants and the boots and the hats and the mittens have gone on for so long that when I look out my window, it's hard to imagine that one day the front lawn will be green instead of white. One day soon we will put away the snow blower and get out the lawn mower, and we might actually be warm instead of perpetually shivering under layers of blankets.

Each morning, Teddy asks me as we hurry from the house to the car when it will be spring or summer. And each morning, I say, "Someday, Teddy, someday." Though even as I say it, and even though I know it is a meteorological fact that spring and then summer will arrive, I am beginning to doubt whether we will ever see it. This winter has been so harsh and so long that it seems like things will never change, like we will constantly be waiting for warmer and brighter days.

The waiting for warmer and brighter—or the illusion of warmer and brighter—has been a recurring theme in my life. It seems that most of my life I have been waiting for something. As a child, I was always waiting for the next holiday, for summer vacation, to graduate from high school. When I was in college, I waited for law school and when I was in law school, I waited to find the right job. I was always waiting to find the right guy, and then when I found him, I waited for him to propose, for the wedding, for the babies. Once the baby came, I waited for him to sleep, to talk, to walk, to start preschool. And for two very long years, I waited to get pregnant with another baby.

Waiting, you might think, would be something I would be good at given all of the experience I have had with waiting. You would be wrong.

I don't do waiting. I fidget and plan all the ways I might be able to speed up this whole waiting thing. I get restless and build up all the ways that this "thing I am waiting for" will be so great, so warm, so bright. I wear myself out with all the fidgeting and planning and building up, and before long, I'm moving around a little slower and heavier. Which, of course, only makes me long for something better, warmer, and brighter.

Even now, as I write, I am waiting. I am waiting to feel settled in this role as writer. I am waiting for this never-ending, god-forsaken winter to be over.

I am waiting, as we are all waiting.

Even when I'm not sure what I'm waiting for, I am waiting. And it has been in this waiting—sometimes a desperate waiting, sometimes a contented waiting—that grace and life and miracles happen. Shauna Niequist writes[30]:

> For me, life was what was happening while I was waiting for my big moment. I was ready for it and believed that the rest of my life would fade into the background, and that my big moment would carry me through life like a lifeboat . . . The Big Moment, unfortunately, is an urban myth . . . Life is a collection of a million, billion moments, tiny little moments and choices, like a handful of luminous, glowing pearls.

So if grace and miracles and the good stuff are all hidden, all tiny and golden and twinkly in the haystack that is the waiting, how do we ever find them?

First, I think we have to stop *looking* and start *seeing, feeling, living,* and *breathing in* all the life that is around us. This is no easy task for some of us; it takes deliberate, constant practice—a spiritual practice, perhaps—until the breathing and the feeling and the living fills us, pushing out the waiting so it can no longer monopolize all that space in our soul.

I've found that it becomes much easier to focus on the living and feeling and breathing in of life when I am doing, serving, and loving. When I am taking the time to check in with friends and family, often and regularly, to ask, "How are you doing, really?" and "What can I help you with?" When I am doing what I can in whatever way I can. When I am praying, whole-heartedly and honestly, for not just my own needs but for those of others. When I am walking the dogs or baking cookies or lighting candles. When I am surrounding myself with beauty and any lush signs of life I can get my hands on.

---

[30] Niequist, *Cold Tangerines*, 16.

Second, and perhaps equally important, driving out the desperation of waiting is a bursting sense of gratitude—a passionate and unequivocal enthusiasm for life, even the parts we have to try really hard just to tolerate, like mountains of snow, infertility treatments, spilled milk, and crushed Cheerios on the couch. Because all of those dull, hard-to-tolerate things make the tiny, golden, twinkly bits of life so much easier to see, like fresh snow, warm sweaters, or hot coffee.

And on top of the gratitude for and the breathing in of life, there is a divine grace that can come in the act of waiting, but it takes a kind of wild and risky faith. Faith that time will move, that circumstances will change, that things will get better, warmer, and brighter. It takes confidence that we are enough just as we are, right where we are. And it takes the wisdom that life is *more* than enough just as it is.

When we package all of that together—the faith, the confidence, and the wisdom—the waiting becomes a little easier, and a little more purposeful. We realize that it is in the constant waiting that we are able to find God and life, love and hope, truth and meaning. And armed with this knowledge, we discover that in spite of the waiting (or maybe *because of* the waiting), we are actually living fully and connecting deeply all along.

Wonder

"He who can no longer pause to wonder and stand rapt in awe, is as good as dead; his eyes are closed."
—Albert Einstein

Flowers in January

"I thank you God for this most amazing day, for the
leaping greenly spirits of trees, and for the blue
dream of sky and for everything which is natural,
which is infinite, which is yes."

—e. e. cummings

When I was young, my paternal grandparents, Stella and
Eugene, would come to stay with us almost every weekend. They
only lived an hour and a half away in Milwaukee, so their frequent
visits were a mainstay in our weekend plans.

The frequency of their visits lent a sort of familiarity to
their presence. Rather than guests, they were quasi-residents, and
all of us went about our business as usual. My dad would still go
into the office on Sunday mornings to do payroll and other
bookkeeping tasks. My mom would run her countless errands. My
sister, brother, and I would go to swim practices and hang out with
our friends. My grandpa would read the newspaper and smoke his
pipe. And my grandma, regardless of the season, would garden.

Gardening, to Grandma, was a year-round activity. At the
first signs of spring, when the snow had barely melted and the
earth was still a sodden mess, she would begin her weekly visits to
Stein's Garden Center to search for bulbs or fertilizer or a new
spade. Summer, obviously, involved constant pruning and
watering. Fall brought raking mounds of leaves that were then used
to cover her beloved roses with a blanket of amber and crimson-
colored, crackly foliage. And even in the winter she would garden,

spending hours poring over the glossy pages of the new Jackson and Perkins catalogue—the gardener's holy book.

There are many things I've inherited from my grandma—her impatience, her outspokenness, her love of crossword puzzles and 500 Rummy, for instance—but her affection for gardening is not among them. I could never understand how she and my dad could spend so many hours tending to flowerbeds and gardens for something that yielded so little in return. Sure, the yard was absolutely gorgeous for two or three months of the year, but their efforts extended throughout all twelve months. And I could never understand why she would spend so many hours taking care of summer's flora when the ground was still swathed in frosty white snow. This was the time for sledding or cuddling up under a blanket with a good book, not for additional chores related to something that wouldn't be achieved for months to come. To me, the investment just did not come close to yielding an adequate return.

But for my grandma, plants and flowers were her life. In fact, gardening is synonymous with my grandma. I cannot think of one without thinking of the other. She visibly came alive when her hands were stained brown, and they were calloused and gritty. She tended to those flowers with an affection and warmth that she sometimes could not provide in her human relationships. Grandma was feisty and funny, but tact and politeness were not always in her repertoire.

Once, when she was cooking dinner for my brother, my sister, and me while my parents were out of town, I asked her if I could have my hamburger without cheese. Thinking that she would happily agree to skip this one extra step in the dinner preparation process, I was shocked when she turned around and said, "What do you think I'm running here, a goddamn restaurant?" She turned back to the stove, added a slice of Velveeta to each burger, and there you had it. If cheeseburgers were on the menu, it was cheeseburgers we would be having.

Grandma led a full and very challenging life, which might have been partly to blame for her lack of manners and civility. Raised dirt poor in rural Pennsylvania, she moved to Milwaukee as a young woman, where she married my grandfather and raised six children, worked as a nurse at a nearby hospital, overcame an alcohol addiction, and learned to drive when she was in her sixties. Let's just say she was too busy surviving to worry much about niceties. When a neighborhood mom paid her a visit one afternoon to chastise her for her teenage sons' inappropriate behavior in sending a pair of black lace panties to the woman's wholesome daughter, Grandma's response was simply, "Do those come in my size, too?"

Maybe it was her calloused upbringing, or maybe it was her way of combating her own personal demons, but whatever the reason, Grandma didn't seem to dwell in the past or worry about the future as other people did. And she never seemed more focused on the now than when she was wrist-deep in a mound of dirt or pampering her beloved roses.

Manners and poise she never quite mastered, but she certainly had the gardening and the nature things figured out, that's for sure. Gardening was her escape from the toils of her human existence, dirt her savior, flowers her soul mates. Perhaps she found grace through plants and flowers because they didn't judge or question or criticize. Perhaps a feeling of oneness with the earth facilitated her spiritual connection with nature. Perhaps she enjoyed gardening simply because it gave her hands something to do to quiet her mind so she could better hear God talking to her. Whatever the reason, gardening was her world, her everything. It was her past, her present, and her future. Gardening was her ever-present now.

Yet despite the pervasiveness of gardening and nature in Grandma's world, I don't think she ever really lost her sense of wonder for it all. In fact, what has always amazed me about those things that bring us a sense of wonder is the way they move beyond the limits of time and location, the way wonder can be as strong today as it was yesterday and will be tomorrow.

Some might say that is the wonder of wonder, I suppose.

In any event, wonder creates sacred connection by linking our past to our present and future. Psychologists, philosophers, writers, religious leaders, and spiritual sages alike—from Eckhart Tolle and Henry David Thoreau to Mahatma Gandhi and Buddha—tell us that to be happy we must live in the present. That we can't dwell in an expired past, nor can we count on an unpredictable future.

But living in the now means occasionally remembering the past. To be at peace in this moment, we sometimes need to spend a few moments honoring the past with truth and authenticity. To cultivate a stronger relationship with the present, we need to spend some time reminiscing about the people who occupy the pages of our past, like my grandma—a strong, vibrant, and flawed woman named Stella who cussed like a truck driver and told dirty jokes, who walked on the beach in just a bra and pair of shorts as a stand-in swimsuit, who made apple dumplings that tasted like a hug. A woman named Stella who loved to garden.

Living in the now also means that we spend a little time hoping for a brighter and warmer future. To more fully enjoy today, we sometimes need to daydream and fantasize about tomorrow, about summer rains and dazzling sunsets. And perhaps to really come alive in the now, to live more fully, we occasionally need to tend to June's vibrant, blooming flowers on a cold January morning.

And wonder at the wonder of it all.

God's Fingers

"Forget not that the earth delights to feel your
bare feet and the winds long to play with your hair."
—Khalil Gibran

As a child, there was really no limit to the ways that nature was infused into my life. I ran through corn stalks taller than my blonde head, helping my parents reap the harvest from our small community garden. I picked crimson, juicy raspberries in the summer with my mom, gorging myself on the luscious fruit until my fingertips were stained red and my belly ached. I ran through prickly grass, barefoot, and jumped into a brown, algae-filled lake at my grandparents' cottage without hesitation. I tasted melting snowflakes on my tongue, threw myself into piles of crinkly leaves, and jumped eagerly into dirty mud puddles.

But then something happened in adulthood. The golden fields of corn became an overlooked backdrop of the rural roads around my hometown, and corn and raspberries were long since relegated to grocery store purchases. The grass became a prickly reminder of summer chores. The lake at my grandparents' cottage began to look greener and slimier, more like a giant mud puddle than a clear swimming pool.

All those earthly wonders that had once provided me with a sense of empowerment began to consist of chores and hassles— snow to be shoveled, leaves to be raked, and mosquitoes to be swatted. The summer too hot, the winter too cold, spring and fall too fleeting to really enjoy.

Like most busy parents, my evenings are filled with all those chores that didn't get done during the day while little hands grabbed at my legs, tiny voices asked for another cup of juice, and energetic bodies needed to be driven to baseball practice. During the day, there are lunches to be made, fights to be quashed, and tantrums to be calmed, so my evenings are filled with dirty dishes, laundry, and e-mails, permission slips and work projects, and all those other things that didn't get done during the day.

Most of the time I thrive on the energy that comes from moving seamlessly from one thing to the next. In fact, if I'm really being honest, I think I use this busyness as a numbing addiction, a high that keeps me feeling productive and needed, without forcing me to open any of my internal boxes or acknowledge the open boxes around me.

During the summer months, my husband loves to sit on our deck and watch the sun settle below the pine trees behind our house. Each night, he calls inside as I putter from one unimportant chore to the next, asking me to join him for a few minutes. And most nights, my response is, "In a minute." He might call again, warning me that the last few moments of twilight are waning, and I typically respond with "in a minute."

Most nights by the time I grab a cup of coffee or glass of wine (depending on how the day had gone) and set down whatever it-can-wait chore I had been tending to, I am too late. Most nights, I miss the sunset, arriving after the sky has turned a deep purplish hue just before it turns black. Most nights, the day's momentum wins out and my self-imposed list of chores deprives me of a few moments of twilight wonder—that brief moment when daylight and darkness dance together before one triumphs over the other.

Most nights, I miss it.

But some nights, I set down my phone, close the computer, and leave the dishes in the sink. Some nights, I beat the stars. Some nights, I make it just in time to see the sky ablaze in fuchsias, auburns, and indigos. Some nights the heavens wink at me, as if to let me in on a little secret.

126

And I almost want to cower in fear of the weightiness of that secret, and hide my face with an uneasy vulnerability.

Sometimes, the weight of wonder is just too much, the awe too overwhelming, for me to grasp. I feel small and unworthy, afraid of its power and potential to pull back the curtain, if only for a moment. Sometimes it's easier to shield myself from a sense of profound wonder by getting busy with laundry and e-mails and games of *Words with Friends*. But all that busying and puttering closes up the boxes and puts lids firmly in place.

The busyness is easier, but the wonder is lovelier. And, honestly, I think we could all use a little less easy and a little more lovely.

In the words of George Washington Carver, "I love to think of nature as an unlimited broadcasting station, through which God speaks to us every hour, if we will only tune in."

I still miss far too many sunsets, but not quite as many. I'm trying to welcome, instead of fear, the sense of wonder.

I'm trying to tune in. Sunsets and stars and swirling snow.

I've been trying to notice the warm sun on my face, a cool breeze through the window, and hot sand through my toes. I've been paying more attention to leaves crunching beneath my feet, snow packed in my hands, and cool rain on my face after a hot summer day.

I've found a radio—now I am just trying to tune in.

Last year, my whole family—husband and sons, my sister and her family, my brother and his wife, and my parents—descended on the greater San Antonio area to celebrate my mom's sixtieth birthday. It was a trip years in the making, with much planning, anticipation, and expectation. In fact, I think we might have spent more time planning and talking about the vacation than we actually spent *on* the vacation. But that's a separate issue entirely.

Like you would expect from a family vacation, the trip certainly had its ups and its downs. It was nice to spend time with family, to leave the winter coats at home, and to gorge ourselves on warm tortilla chips and spicy salsa. But traveling with young children is always a challenge, as is traveling with a group as large as ours, and by the end of the trip my husband and I were pretty worn out.

One day near the end of the trip, Matt and I were feeling particularly exhausted. We were looking forward to returning home to get a bit of a vacation from our vacation, so to speak. We pulled into the hotel parking lot after a long afternoon outing, our kids dozing in the backseat. Being the technology and social media addict that I am, I was glancing at my iPhone as the car turned into an open parking space. And then . . . I looked up.

It was one of those seemingly insignificant occurrences that are often overlooked. One of those moments when if you aren't careful it can pass you by without the slightest pause for notice. One of those exhibitions of the Divine that is so fleeting that you might not even realize you had just been given a rare glimpse behind the curtain.

Right before me, through the front window, were ghostly streams of wispy sunlight cutting through the hazy afternoon clouds, dancing upon the grassy hills that surrounded us. Ordinarily I would have noticed the sight, albeit with little fanfare or reverence, and quickly moved on to the next activity, shuffling our children inside, preoccupied with what was next. But something about this moment made me stop and stare a few moments longer.

My husband noticed the sight as well, and for a few minutes we sat still and quiet, staring straight ahead, allowing the moment to wiggle its way into the nooks and crannies of our hearts just a little bit. For a few minutes, we forgot about the bundles of obligations that awaited us back home. We forgot about the relentless job pressures, the unceasing exhaustion, and the oppressive unknowns. We forgot about the daily hassles, the prickly anxieties, and the everyday challenges that can pile up until they become mountains of burden.

I stared ahead and allowed myself to not just *see* those translucent rays of light, but to *feel* them on me and in me and around me, like God's fingers reaching down to caress my face, like the resilient twine of a giant safety net enveloping me, like a thousand flashlights of comfort leading the way home.

Loveliness. Wonder.

I'm not sure if my husband felt the spiritual significance of this moment as profoundly as I did, or if he merely enjoyed a few moments of quiet before the madness of family travel began again. But when I glanced over at him, I saw a slight, but unmistakable, trace of contentment and peace.

Then again, maybe his face was simply mirroring the voice inside my soul.

Stillness

"A moment of sacred silence is our cosmic
reset button."
—Marianne Williamson

I have one of those busy, active minds that jumps from thought to thought, task to task, worry to worry. Restlessness, stress, or anxiety might be good terms to characterize me psychologically. "Monkey mind" if I'm feeling very New Age or Zen about it. Or jittery, jumpy, unsettled, and impatient if I'm being more practical about it. I'm constantly on the go, moving from one activity to the next, and if there's nothing next, I will come up with something.

As quickly as my body moves from one thing to the next, my mind moves even more quickly. While eating breakfast, I'm thinking about what's for lunch; during lunch, I'm wondering what I will make for dinner. My to-do list is planned out weeks in advance, with empty days quickly filled; the weekend is scheduled as soon as Monday morning hits. And while all of the go-go-going and jumping from branch to branch does help me get a lot done, it also leaves me feeling utterly exhausted and more than a little disconnected. Days and weeks hurry past in a flurry of chores and activities and scheduled plans; minutes and hours speed by as I jump from one worry to the next. Each day blurs into the next, without pause or a chance to breathe, and before I know it, years have been erased from my life.

As a child, however, as busy as the week might have been, there was no mistaking when Sunday rolled around. Sunday was so clearly different from any other day. The morning began early, but

131

was quiet and subdued. After returning from church service, the house would quickly fill with the rich smells of a decadent breakfast, which might even include store-bought Danish if we were lucky. The entire family gathered around the table for a long, lazy breakfast before retreating to our respective corners for a few hours.

If my grandparents were in town, dinner was a heavy mid-afternoon meal carefully timed to coincide with halftime of the Packers game—one of the only times the television was on during the day.

Sunday moved on a special schedule, with a cadence and rhythm all its own. The day was slower, quieter, calmer. It was sacred.

But somehow, somewhere, between then and now, things changed. Weekends became about chores and errands, laundry and grocery shopping, e-mails and work projects. Since I do most of my writing while the boys are sleeping or otherwise occupied, Sunday became just another workday for me. And if, heaven forbid, I did find myself with a few moments of quiet, well, I could always count on my iPhone, the television, or the Internet to distract me and keep me from dealing with the uncomfortable and unfamiliar *stillness*.

About a year ago, while I was reading *The Sabbath World* by Judith Shulevitz with the Spirituality Girls, I realized just how much I was longing for a day of rest (or even just a few minutes of rest). I realized I had become so completely dependent on technology and the go-go-going of my multi-tasking lifestyle that I didn't even know how to be alone with myself or how to navigate a sense of stillness. As a result, I had lost (and was continuing to lose) a sense of sacred connection to family, to self, and to the Divine.

The thought of following *Shabbat*—a Sabbath day—was both exhilarating and absolutely terrifying, which, of course, was precisely the reason I needed to do it. I read more about the origins of the Christian Sabbath and the traditional rules of Jewish *Shabbat*.

I considered my lifestyle, my family's needs, and the practical implications of following the Sabbath. And I took a long, hard look at the things creating the disconnections.

Ultimately, I decided what I desperately needed was a day—or any period of time, really—focused on rest, reflection, and reconnection. So I created my own kind of Sabbath or *Shabbat*. A modern-day Sabbath, if you will. Unlike the Sabbath or *Shabbat*, there are no hard and fast rules; rather, it is more personal and intentional. It is about setting aside a time to settle into the stillness, to focus on what I have instead of searching for something new. It's a time to disconnect from work and technology to reconnect with family and friends and self, and a time to quiet the external noise so I can hear my own internal voice.

Basically, it is an attempt at internal stillness, an intentional effort to "turn off and tune in." For me, that means no iPhone, no television, no computer, no Internet. It means rest and music and church, prayer and meditation, time with family, and time alone. It also means several failed attempts at patience and a jittery discomfort with this new and very foreign feeling of stillness. It means listening to and dealing with squabbles between the boys instead of turning away from the situation by checking my e-mail. It means constant reminders that I do not need to order new shoes online *right this instant*, that I do not need to Google "vegetarian soup recipes" *right now*, and that I do not need to check Facebook *today*. It means a little more preparation, coordination, and communication so nothing slips through the cracks and necessary obligations are covered.

Of course, in our technology-driven society, it also means a few inconveniences and hassles. Since I'm not available by cell phone, I can be difficult to reach, and meeting my sister at the zoo can become more difficult since I can't just text when I get there. It means being somewhere when you say you're going to be there. And it means waiting and waiting and waiting.

In today's day and age of instant gratification and constant communication, it feels strange to force myself to wait and to give myself some time and space from the constant influx of information. The Internet and smartphones make it possible for us to feed most of our wants and needs now, whether it's looking for a recipe, buying a new swimsuit, or checking the weather. Technology has also made it easier than ever to numb our emotions and distract us from anxieties. Social media—Facebook, Twitter, Pinterest—television, twenty-four-hour "news" coverage, and blogs all give us an easy outlet for distraction so we don't have to endure discomfort, whether within ourselves or among others. But a constant reliance on technology to do everything *right now* has the potential to feed our impatience and self-importance. An over-reliance on technology as a means of communication has the potential to trivialize our relationships, and the use of technology as a coping mechanism to numb our emotions has the potential to prevent personal growth and development.

Unplugging for one day (or a few hours) each week is a reminder that life unfolds on a timetable not always within my control. By removing the distractions, being still, and clearing internal space, I am slowly learning to become comfortable with my own discomfort to gain a certain depth of self-awareness and to figure out how to work through, not around, problems. I am learning to reconnect with myself, my family, and the Spirit. As Shulevitz wrote in *Sabbath World*, "There is no better point of entry to the religious experience than the Sabbath, for all its apparent ordinariness. *Because* of its ordinariness. The extraordinariness of the Sabbath lies in its being commonplace . . . the day all about getting connected."[31]

---

[31] Judith Shulevitz, introduction to *The Sabbath World: Glimpses of a Different Order of Time*, (New York: Random House, 2011), xxiii.

The remarkable thing is that there is a slowing of time in the stillness and the quiet and the waiting, almost like capturing time in a bottle. Time is a funny thing. It seems to morph and expand and contract, with some days slogging along, and then in the blink of an eye, a month, a year, or a decade has passed and we are reeling from the loss of our human time. But what good does it do to speed it up with our go-go-going, e-mailing, texting, Facebooking, and the instant gratifications? What good does it do to disconnect and numb ourselves from the anxieties? When we disconnect or numb the pain, we also disconnect and numb the joy.

After I've turned off my cell phone, let the withdrawal jitters pass, and stopped worrying about all the things I might be missing, there is a silent freedom that feels almost rebellious. By separating one day from the frenzied blur of the remaining six, by disconnecting from the frenetic pace of technology to reconnect with the sacredly simple, and by settling into the stillness and the quiet and the waiting, I have accomplished the impossible. I have actually *slowed* time. I have touched it and smelled it and tasted it.

And in all of that waiting and stillness and time-slowing, I just might be lifting the lid off a few boxes as well.

A Symphony of Sounds

"After silence, that which comes nearest to
expressing the inexpressible is music."
—Aldous Huxley

One of the very first things I do each morning after I've gone to the bathroom and brushed my teeth, but before I pour myself a cup of coffee or let the dogs out, is press the "play" button on my iPod speaker. The music varies. Some days I choose a collection of Broadway show tunes, others an eclectic mix of trendy Indie music like Local Natives and Grimes, and on some mornings it's a classic mix of pop/rock songs by Elton John, Journey, or Billy Joel. In any event, from the time I wake up until the moment my head hits the pillow at night (and sometimes even long after I have fallen asleep), music is playing non-stop at my house.

If I could have one talent, it would be to sing. Unfortunately, I can't carry a tune to save my life and, aside from a few years of piano lessons, I'm not what you would call "musically inclined." Nonetheless, something inexplicable and almost divine happens to me when I hear certain music.

There are times when the spiritual energy a certain song or rhythm creates is so strong and uncontrollable that my body moves and sounds escape from my mouth. Some people might call this dancing or singing, but I'm hesitant to call it that. Dancing implies some kind of rhythmic movement, and singing implies a melody, both of which are lacking when I'm doing these things.

The right kind of music (which is, of course, a matter of personal preference) captures the essence of sacred connection. Music lives and breathes and moves, and it has a way of touching our heart, mind, voice, body, and soul all at the same time. Like any good art, music has the ability to speak to us in ways that words alone cannot. Music digs into our soul's pores and leaves us forever changed. It touches our senses in a way that few things can so that all those inexplicable and unknown feelings suddenly become palpable, understandable, and knowable in an intimate way that creates an almost visceral response. When I first sang "Lean on Me" in church, with our congregation holding hands, tears streamed down my face. "Breath Me" is like a meditative chant, the African hymn "Siyahamba" lifts my spirit as I clap along, and just about anything by Passion Pit makes the blood dance through my veins.

When I worshiped at Micah's Porch, a small liberal church community in downtown Chicago, we often sang the Foo Fighters' "Learn to Fly" to begin Sunday services. While this might seem like an odd musical selection—or even a blasphemous choice for some more conservative religious folks—that song, which I had previously heard thousands of times on the radio, took on a whole new meaning for me. In that setting, surrounded by my church community, "Learn to Fly" became a connective life force, a spiritual energy, and a holy hymn that spoke to my soul in ways that no minister's words could ever do. And by choosing that song and making music a central focus of Micah's Porch worship services, Pastor Dave showed us what people have been trying to say since the beginning of time: music has a soul all its own. In the right setting, and with the right frame of mind, music has a way of connecting its soul to our own, filling us with an almost pulsating sense of awe. It wasn't necessarily the particular song or its lyrics that made the music so transformative and impactful; rather it was the juxtaposition of the secular within the sacred, the intersection of art and life, the coming together of the everyday with the Divine.

Music, at its most basic level, is about connecting melodies with lyrics and notes with chords. On a more profound level, music is about a connection with the Divine. Music, like all art, opens boxes and connects. Art—whether music, painting, photography, or poetry—is about connecting the creator with the recipient, the source with the beneficiary, the Divine with the earthly, and the spiritual with the physical.

Music has been called the "universal language of mankind." Hans Christian Andersen once said, "Where words fail, music speaks." Shauna Niequist wrote, "Art slips past our brains straight into our bellies. It weaves itself into our thoughts and feelings and the open spaces in our souls, and it allows us to live more and say more and feel more. Great art says the things we wished someone would say out loud, the things we wish we could say out loud."[32]

Not only does music speak the unspoken language, it also touches the untouched places. It makes us feel things—fear, gratitude, love, vulnerability—at an intensity and acuity with which we are ordinarily unaccustomed. Within music lies an intrinsic understanding of that which cannot be understood or explained. Music cracks us open and fills the empty spaces with feelings so big and bold that our spoken language is just not equipped to handle it. Music fills our hearts, minds, senses, and very beings with a beauty that can only be created by a wholly personal connection with the Spirit—a connection the musician facilitates.

Famed writer Stephen King calls this telepathy. "All the arts depend upon telepathy to some degree,"[33] he writes. He goes on to explain that when he writes a description of something—say, a rabbit in a cage with the number eight marked on it, for instance—there is a meeting of the minds between the writer and the reader, albeit one with a lot of flexibility and room for interpretation.

---

[32] Niequist, *Cold Tangerines*, 227.
[33] King, *On Writing*, 95.

But if writing is a meeting-of-the-minds kind of telepathy, as King suggests (while admitting to an obvious prejudice toward writing as the purest form of art-induced telepathy), for me, music creates a meeting-of-the-souls kind of telepathy—a connection that cannot subsist on words or sounds alone, but on words, sounds, vibrations, feelings, emotions, and . . . well . . . you get the idea. It's a kind of all-consuming connection between the music creator and the music receiver.

For instance, to me, the music that Justin Vernon creates with Bon Iver is like stepping into some kind of spiritual shower in which my soul is washed clean and rejuvenated in a way that I cannot describe, only feel. For my husband Matt, Vernon's music just makes him want to take a nap. Over the years, there are many ways in which my and Matt's musical tastes have influenced each other. I have learned to enjoy indie electronica a bit more, and he has learned to sing along to folksy singer-songwriters from time to time. But even taking into account our shared musical preferences, there is a highly personal, almost visceral connection that we each feel with music and its creator—a connection that cannot be replicated or duplicated, or described for that matter.

The art of creating sacred connection is all about opening ourselves up and standing back in reverence and awe and amazement, and then tying the frayed threads and knotted edges together to create a life of beauty, meaning, and fulfillment. And this is no easy task. There are no one-size-fits-all instructions, no rules or guidelines. Opening ourselves up and then standing back as the messes spill out of the neat and clean boxes we created can be overwhelming and confusing at times. And then holding ourselves open, enduring the discomfort and terrifying fear that comes in the rough-and-tumble world of open-hearted living, can be almost intolerable at times. I, for one, have to constantly fight the urge to close myself off, put up walls, and separate. But as intimidating and dubious as living a grace-full and open-hearted life can be at times, music is like soft sand to carry us through the journey. Music is a warm embrace, a shoulder to cry on, a friend telling us, "Hush now, you're not alone." Music can be a stadium full of fans cheering us as we muddle our way through unchartered territory, a quiet prayer in the dark corners of the night, or a frame for the sweet joys and bitter sorrows of our life.

Art mirrors our heart and mind and soul. It speaks the unspeakable with depth, clarity, and perception. And it makes us feel a little less alone. It is nothing short of divine and holy.

As I write this, I am listening to one of my "writing" playlists on my iPhone. Songs by Bon Iver, Jimi Hendrix, and Sade echo through the room. Some of the tunes are mere background noise, like gentle stretches before a workout; others are a little more like acupuncture, striking a nerve and cutting deep with a sensation that reverberates throughout my entire being, leaving me exhausted and vulnerable. It is at these times, however, when the art of music stirs up such raw and tender emotions, that I feel the most whole, pure, and connected to myself, my writing, and my world. And *that*, I suppose, is the real wonder of music. Not only does make us feel more intensely, but it makes us feel safe, protected, and just a little bit closer to God while doing so.

Music transports us to another place, pulls back the curtain a bit, and transcends the random or chaotic goings-on around us. And couldn't we all use a little more transcendence, a little less chaotic, if only for a few moments?

Star Stuff

"The body is our general medium for
having a world."
—Maurice Merleau-Ponty

Like just about every person I know, I have a lot on my plate. I am a full-time at-home parent. I also have a part-time job as a freelance legal writer. Then there is the part-part-time hobby that is my blog. And my part-part-part-time dream of writing this book. Now I've never been very good at math, but if I add up all those jobs and hobbies and dreams, there's a lot more time involved in that to-do list than hours in a day. But, like I said, I was never good at math.

Fortunately, I don't need math. I just need the List.

The List is a finely tuned and well-oiled machine, one that thrives on the *click-click-click* of progress in the form of chores checked off and projects completed. It operates on a steady diet of coffee, catnaps, and chocolate to keep the machine running smoothly.

I tend to take for granted that my body is physically responsible for keeping the *click-click-click* of the List humming. My fingers move up and down to tap the keys as I write. My legs carry me throughout the day, to the dry cleaners, the gym, and the grocery store, and they happily tuck up underneath me at night. My arms lift gallons of milk and little boys who need a hug after they fall off their bike. Inside, my heart pumps blood, my lungs move air in and out and around, and my stomach converts food into energy. And, most days, all of this activity and energy and life goes on within me without much thought or deliberation on my part.

Truthfully, the high functionality and inner workings of my body—the way that it carries me through my day so I can adhere to the List, tuck my boys into bed at night, and then curl up next to my husband—all go on without much thought or appreciation.

Until things break down a bit, there's a kink in the system, or a glitch in the hard-wiring.

A few weeks ago, our family came down with a full-blown, five-alarm stomach virus. Within a matter of hours, we were all vomiting, moaning, and begging for mercy. Needless to say, the List for that week went out the window, and while I don't believe in hell, I'm pretty sure if there were a hell that it would consist of an all-family case of the stomach flu.

Fortunately, the illness was relatively short-lived and we were all back on our feet, for the most part, within a few days. And once I was back on my feet, eating solid foods again, I felt like Wonder Woman conquering the world.

But why did it take a raging stomach virus to make me appreciate the amazingness of the human body? I don't for one second presume to equate our brief stay in the dredges of the Norovirus with anything truly horrific like cancer, paralysis, or multiple sclerosis, but I will admit that after spending the better part of a few days either vomiting or cleaning up vomit, I have a new (or renewed) respect for the wonders of a properly functioning human body.

Most of the time I take my body for granted. Even though I was an athlete for twelve years, most of my life has been spent chastising my body for being too this or too that. Too jiggly or too flat. Too big in some places; too small in other places.

As a teen, I was scrawny, flat-chested, and boyish. I wanted a more feminine body, one that was curvier and softer. As an adult, after I stopped swimming umpteen hours a day, I got that curvier and softer body I'd wanted, except by that time I wanted the thin body back.

One spring evening toward the end of college, I stood in my bedroom, my sister seated cross-legged on my bed, in front of an open closet and a full-length mirror. I was packing for a trip to Florida the next day and piles of shorts and tank tops were scattered across the floor. After tugging on shorts in various shapes and sizes, and sucking in my stomach to clasp the button on each pair, I looked at myself in the mirror with angry tears in my eyes.

"Nothing fits," I cried.

"What about the pair of yellow denim shorts? Those seemed pretty good. Or do you have any sundresses you could try?" Carrie offered feebly. She knew there was no time to shop for new clothes as much as she knew that buying bigger clothes was not the solution I was looking for.

I tore off the shorts, turned away from the mirror, and collapsed on the bed.

"You'll find something to wear. You always look beautiful," Carrie said, knowing there was nothing more she could do or say at that moment.

I lay on my bed for a while, feeling the hatred for my body reach new and uncharted heights. That weekend, as I stuffed myself into too-small shorts and too-tight dresses, my hatred morphed into something bitter and controlling and judgmental. Rules and restrictions were the answer, I told myself. If I eat nothing, maybe I can get rid of the excess thigh jiggle and erase some of the physical shame.

But over time with each calorie counted, each meal skipped, and each pound lost, the hatred only grew. Before long, I had lost a significant amount of weight and was in the throes of a full-blown eating disorder. And I had never hated my body more. Food and exercise consumed my every waking minute. I felt anxious before meals, and anxious after meals. And I always felt hungry, drained, and empty. Instead of praising my body for pumping blood and oxygenating air and providing life, I blamed it for its various needs and wants and limitations.

As a result, I became increasingly more disconnected from my body, largely because I expected my body to be like those boxes at the top of my hallway closet—pretty, predictable, and controllable. In fact, I think it was because of this disconnection with my body that I was able to criticize, abuse it, and take it for granted. It didn't much matter to me that my body—an intricate collection of cells, tissues, nerves, and organs working in unison—was a functioning and highly productive mechanism upon which I was utterly dependent. My body was something I wanted to control and manipulate. By tightening the walls around myself, by shrinking and pulling myself inward, I thought I could separate, package, and hide the jumbled-up messes stirring around inside.

Despite the fact that I had been an athlete for twelve years, never during those years did I pause to appreciate my body just for the sheer fact that it gave me life and carried me through my day, let alone that it was able to train and compete. There is, I think, a natural tendency to take the status quo—heart beating, lungs filling with air, nerves firing, muscles flexing—for granted, to just assume that this is the way it has been and this is the way that it will always be. We don't pay much attention to the miraculous process that allows us to take in food, digest it, use what we need, and get rid of what we don't until there's a mishap somewhere along the line. When I wake up in the morning, my first thought is usually, *Sweet baby Jesus, I really need more sleep, and my back has a knot, and I feel really bloated, and I think I pulled a muscle I didn't know I had.* It's not, *Thank God I'm awake and breathing and feeling and living.*

Over the course of several months, and with a lot of love and support, I slowly dug my way out of the bowels of anorexia. I stopped hating my body, my skin and bones, my cellulite and fat rolls, and my nerves and muscles quite so much.

I wish I could say I learned to *love* my body then, but it hasn't been until recently that the concept of self-care and mind-body connection made any sense to me. And it is still something I struggle with from time to time. I've recovered from the eating disorder. But like any recovering addict, I suppose, each day is a constant fight not to criticize, judge, or punish my body and myself.

I would like to say I learned to appreciate my body when I was pregnant and after I gave birth (I had grown a person after all), but I didn't. I took for granted that I had become pregnant in the first place, and hated just about everything that came along with it: the nausea, the swollen ankles, the skin rashes, the sore breasts, the varicose veins, the wide ass, the heartburn, the leaky nipples, the hormonal highs and lows, the poochy belly, the weakened bladder, and a whole bunch of other things you wouldn't want to read about. Throughout my first pregnancy, I tended to focus on all the ways my body was weaker than it had been before and, after Jackson was born, I was consumed by all the ways my body was worse than it had been before his birth. My boobs were big and sore. I had a persistent five-months-pregnant belly pooch. And I may or may not have peed my pants. In public. More than once.

Just like we often take for granted the air breathing and blood pumping and food digesting our bodies do until a problem arises, I don't know if a woman can ever really appreciate the wonder of pregnancy and childbirth until things don't go as planned.

As teens and young adults we try so hard *not* to get pregnant and then, at some point, we decide that *now* is the time. And we expect that it will happen just like that. When Jackson was about fifteen months old, Matt and I decided it was time for another child. We had made our way out of the fog of infancy. Jackson was walking, talking, and sleeping through the night, and we both felt ready to handle the whirlwind that pregnancy and a new baby bring into a family. We knew I might not get pregnant immediately, but there seemed to be an unspoken assumption that within a few months I would be pregnant, and within a year or so Jackson would have a sibling. It had happened once, after all, so why wouldn't it happen again?

We did not expect, nor were we prepared for, a years-long struggle with infertility and three miscarriages. Without getting into the nitty-gritty, my body wasn't able to get pregnant as easily as before and, when it did, it was ill equipped to maintain the pregnancy. Basically, there was a glitch in the system. Everything I had taken for granted when pregnant with Jackson, everything I had assumed would go as it should, was flipped upside down. I no longer expected to get pregnant and stay pregnant; instead, it was just the opposite. I expected my life would become one long saga of pregnancy and miscarriage, pregnancy and miscarriage, until Matt and I eventually surrendered.

One June morning I saw the two pink lines on the pregnancy stick again. Cautiously optimistic, I made an appointment with my doctor right away (by that time I was under the close watch of highly trained fertility specialists). Yes, they said, I was in fact pregnant.

But by the next morning, it appeared I was not.

There are certain calm and patient women. There are women who can eat only one cookie and not an entire sleeve of Oreos, or can take one pregnancy test and not buy the entire stock at Jewel or the Dollar Store. I am *not* one of these women. Over the course of a couple of days, I peed on enough sticks to cause E.P.T.'s stock to go up a hundred points, each one of them with one glaringly ugly single pink line. Again, my body didn't do what I had wanted it to do, what other women's bodies were able to do so easily.

When I went back to the doctor a few days later to discuss "next steps," they told me I was surprisingly still pregnant. (Turns out those pee sticks aren't 100 percent accurate—who knew?) Over the next few months, we saw our fertility doctor on a weekly basis, each visit confirming that I was, in fact, still pregnant. At each visit, I expected to learn that something had gone awry, that my body wasn't sustaining the pregnancy as it should because by that point there was no more *should*, there was only loss. At each visit, I stared in utter amazement at the tiny little bean that, despite the odds, continued to grow and thrive inside my body.

At my twelve-week appointment, I sat on the doctor's table and sobbed, unable to control the overwhelming awe and joy I felt for the human body, for *my* body. The same body I had abused and criticized and condemned. The same body I had taken for granted when functioning properly and chastised when it didn't. The same body from which I had separated myself, treating it more like a heap of clay to mold than a divine machine to be revered. My body had done this. Amazing. Absolutely amazing.

As I sat there sobbing in my hospital gown, with my doctor asking in a concerned motherly voice, "Are you okay? Is everything all right?" the only thing I could think was, *Why isn't every pregnant woman crying in wonder and awe? Why aren't we all sobbing joyfully over the amazingness of life?* Lying on that hospital table, hearing the tiny *thrum-thrum-thrum* of my new baby's heartbeat inside my belly, I began my very slow journey of connection and appreciation for my body and all of its gifts.

Though I'm more of a word person than a science person, I do know that the wonders of the human body are without measure. It can make and grow people. Amazing. It can carry grocery bags and diapers bags and fifty-pound seven-year-olds who are too tired to walk. Amazing. It takes in oxygen, moves it around and converts it into something completely different, and then uses that something different to give life to other things. Amazing. It gets cut, bleeds, scars, and then heals. Absolutely amazing.

As if that weren't amazing enough, our bodies are made of the stuff of stars. Carl Sagan wrote in *Cosmic Connection*, "Our Sun is a second- or third-generation star. All of the rocky and metallic material we stand on, the iron in our blood, the calcium in our teeth, the carbon in our genes were produced billions of years ago in the interior of a red giant star. We are made of star-stuff."[34] Can you believe that? We are actually made of the stuff of stars. Amazing, I tell you. Absolutely amazing.

I have made significant improvements in terms of self-care and body image in the past fifteen years, largely due to improved self-esteem and the love of a man who never stops telling me I'm beautiful. Nonetheless, loving my body for the wondrous working machine that it is continues to be a struggle. I still pinch my belly a bit too much and get cranky if the number on the scale is higher this week than last. I still get frustrated when I come down with a cold or catch a stomach virus or pee my pants (hypothetically, of course). I see too many wrinkles and laugh lines. I wish my body were bigger in some places and smaller in others. I rarely leave the house without a layer of creamy foundation and some under-eye concealer. I still keep the List and get annoyed when something, whether internal or external, causes it to get derailed.

But what I am finding is that those mornings when I breathe in a tiny moment of awe for all that my body—with its flabby skin and brittle bones—is able to do, when I am able to say "wow" for the wonder that is life, I free up just enough space and mental energy to appreciate my body for its capabilities and its connection to the cosmic whole. But when I am consumed with the laugh lines and forehead wrinkles, the cellulite and the belly rolls, the achy knees and funky-looking toenails, my mind and spirit gets a little murky and clouded, and there isn't any room left for anything except an acute awareness of lacking. The physical vanity and flaw-spotting blocks out any possibility of gratitude, let alone a mind-body-spirit connection.

I'm not ready to toss out my makeup bag, the hair cream, or the self-tanning lotion. I will continue to color my hair from

---

[34] Carl Sagan, *Cosmic Connection: An Extraterrestrial Perspective*, (1973; reprint, New York: Cambridge University Press, 2000), 190.

time to time, exercise daily, and try to eat healthy. There is nothing wrong with wanting to look and feel our best. We're trying to feel more connected, after all, not *invisible*, for goodness sake. The key, I think, is to practice self-love along with the self-care, to appreciate how amazing our bodies are just as they are, and to honor the worth of our physicality as part of something bigger and more amazing than the achy knees, bad backs, droopy eyelids, and belly pooches.

Physical temples. Divine machines. A medium for the world. Star-stuff.

Or as the genius Anne Lamott said, *WOW*.

Quantum Physics

"The health of the eye seems to demand a horizon.
We are never tired, so long as we can
see far enough."
— Ralph Waldo Emerson

I was a child of the eighties and I still remember our first family computer. It was a big, hulking machine that took up half the kitchen table. There was no Internet yet, so it was basically just an extra big typewriter with a magic eraser function and blinking lights.

It sat in the basement, where it was out of sight for the most part, because who wants to stare at such an ugly behemoth of a machine all the time? And, really, there was no other place to house such a big machine. So there it sat in the basement where my sister, my brother, and I would fight for screen time to type up whatever school assignment we were working on or play *Where in the World is Carmen San Diego?*

I felt so modern and worldly typing up book reports and essays for English composition on this computer, like I was part of some elite team of scientists or tech experts whose work was given instant credibility because it was typed on an MS-DOS computer with green illuminated letters. Never mind that I had (and still have) no idea was DOS stands for or that I didn't speak computer; I felt innovative and fresh.

Once I was in college, the Internet had taken off and e-mail had become fairly commonplace, not in the smartphone, text message, conversational kind of way that e-mail is used now, but in more of a once-a-week kind of way. Although I consider myself to be somewhat computer literate now (I know "cookies" are more than just gooey treats with chocolate chips in them, and I know a "browser" isn't someone sifting through racks at Nordstrom or perusing the shelves at Barnes & Noble), this whole "Internet" thing still floors me. I mean, how is it possible that the words I type on my computer screen in Chicago can instantly be transmitted to a cousin who lives in Florida, my sister in Wisconsin, or a friend in California? Remarkable. And how are words and thoughts and ideas—all of these intangible things—traveling through cyber-optic wires with the push of a button? Astonishing. And how can some scrawny, pierced teenager halfway around the world hack into my computer and send out e-mails to all of my contacts with links to strange websites for Viagra and weight-loss pills? Absolutely incredible.

I know I must sound like I am about a hundred years old, a little old lady sitting in my rocking chair, sipping tea, and marveling at the telephone or color television, but the Internet still seems like some kind of voodoo magic to me. And don't even get me started on iPhones, the Cloud, or Google Glass.

A couple of years ago, scientists discovered this thing called the Higgs boson, which apparently was a pretty big deal in the scientific community. As I have said, I'm more of a word person than a science person, but from what I can understand the Higgs bosom is basically this mass-less subatomic field that connects all particles and gives those particles mass. To use non-science people lingo, it's kind of like a little kid pulling a sled through three feet of fresh snow or Kim Kardashian trying to move through a teeming mob of paparazzi. The Higgs bosom clamors around particles—the little kid with a sled or Kim Kardashian—making it more difficult to move and thereby giving them mass.

Until now, scientists have been stumped about how subatomic particles—protons, neutrons, and electrons—acquire mass and what holds these particles together. In other words, they

154

didn't know what made Kim Kardashian so popular (something I'm still trying to figure out) or caused the kid to pull the sled so slowly. About fifty years ago, Peter Higgs and some other really smart people came up with this idea that there must be some unknown attractive force holding all these particles together. But until they confirmed the existence of the Higgs boson, they weren't quite sure what that "thing" was. They weren't sure why it took a kid pulling a sled through the snow about fifteen minutes just to get across the backyard or why Kim Kardashian was so popular. When they confirmed the existence of this teensy-tiny, *subatomic* particle, however, then they had their answer. It was the Higgs boson, the snow, and the swarms of paparazzi that were responsible.

The existence of subatomic particles, let alone mass-less subatomic particles, is something my mind has considerable difficulty grasping. My mind just cannot understand the miniscule nature of its existence, its mass-less existence, or the profoundly technical methods scientists used to discover it.

Of course, a discovery with the magnitude of the Higgs boson was not without controversy. Some scientists questioned its discovery and instead thought it might be a mix of particles, and not just the Higgs, that was actually discovered. *It's snow AND sand AND rocks* that slowed the kid with the sled, they said. *It's paparazzi AND fans AND the media* swarming around the reality star turned celebrity.

The media wanted to latch on to its controversial nickname as the "God particle," though scientists were quick to point out that this trendy moniker holds no real significance. In fact, the Nobel Laureate who is credited with introducing the "God particle" admitted that he originally referred to the Higgs boson as the "goddamn particle" due to its elusiveness. Religious groups used the discovery of the "God particle," or a mass-less energy force that ties the universe together, as support for the existence of God, whereas atheists argued that the discovery supported a conclusion that the universe was created solely as a result of scientific principles at work, and not by God.

When it comes to scientific issues like subatomic particles and the Internet, I'm fairly content to remain a little naïve about all of it. When I send an e-mail to my husband at work asking him to pick up milk on the way home, I'm happy to accept the mystery of how words on a screen at my house in the suburbs can reach his computer in downtown Chicago without understanding the how or why of it. I don't need to know whether the discovery of the "God particle" proves or disproves God's existence, whether there was a creator or a source, or whether it was random chance or a godly plan. What I do know, however, is that this thing called the Higgs boson is something that until a few years ago had been unknown, or at least unprovable, to even the most renowned scientific minds. A few years ago, it was just a concept; now it's provable. What had previously been unknown will now become a mainstay of modern-day physics. Just like what is unknown today is yet to be discovered tomorrow.

So much of what we now know about the nature of the universe has eluded us for much of humanity's existence simply because we lacked the technology or the intelligence or the creativity to see it. Until half a century ago, the moon was just this big rock in the sky, and now scientists can see galaxies that are several light-years away.

There is so much that is smaller than we can see, and so much that is bigger than our minds can grasp. There always will be. It is mind-boggling and absolutely *amazing* to think of the yet-to-be-discovered possibilities that might exist, things that we just can't see or know or understand right now—other mass-less energy fields like the Higgs boson, angels, other galaxies, God or gods, other planets, spirits, other universes. Does our inability to see them mean they don't exist? Does our inability to understand them make them any less real? Does our inability to explain them make them any less amazing?

Maybe. But maybe not.

Maybe a reverence for the mysteries of life, an open mind, and willingness to be amazed at the known, as well as the unknown, is what makes all those indecipherable small things and big things so magical in the first place. Maybe the answers aren't found in scientific research or mathematical equations, nor through telescopes or under microscopes. Maybe the answers are found in a quest for knowledge and truth coupled with a humble awe for the sacred unknown and infinite holy mysteries.

Sometimes when Matt and I are feeling extra brave, we will broach the subject of "what we don't know." Things like the stars and the universe and whether plants have feelings. Heck, we might even mix in a little talk about spirituality, religion, and philosophy if we're feeling really adventurous. Matt likes to take the energy fields and quantum physics approach. I, on the other hand, like to focus on the mystical and the Divine. Things like the way the moon might influence winemaking or whether dolphins fall in love. Honestly, the phrase "quantum physics" kind of makes my head spin. Nonetheless, we humor each other. I listen to him wax on about subatomic particles and a "grid of energy"; he listens to me talk about reincarnation and our spiritual connection to trees. Usually, these conversations are an entertaining exchange of ideas about the mysteries of life. Other times, the discussion is too deep and heady for me. I get overwhelmed with the unknown and the possibilities; the uncertainty sparks an emotional, almost instinctual, response and the conversation ends with tears (mine) or not so subtle segue into a new conversation about baseball (his).

For some reason, these hidden mysteries—the things that are too big or too small to see, let alone fully comprehend—often stir up passionate and visceral reactions. There is a tendency to label science and religion as inherently incompatible, but really science, religion, and even philosophy are more alike than they are different; they are each just ways of trying to answer the same existential questions: *Where did we come from, and why are we here? What is the purpose of life, and what does it all mean?*

Science and spirituality don't have to be incompatible. In fact, I think that they depend on one another in order to embark on an authentic search for truth. They both require humility and curiosity, an open mind and an open heart, exploring what we don't know, and connecting the dots of what we do know. Our universe is full of existences and actualities that are, as yet, undetected. There is something magically divine in reveling in the mystery of the unknowns lurking within and among us. And when we celebrate the unknown, when we open our minds to the infinite possibilities, we give ourselves the gift of faith that whatever uncertainties and tattered pieces lie within us and around us, they can be tied together. Even if we can't put them together right now.

But maybe someday.

What's Next?

"If there are no dogs in heaven, then when I die I want to go where they went."
—Will Rogers

My uncle died on a Thursday in July, my paternal grandpa on a Sunday in November, my other grandpa on a Friday in July, and my grandma on a Tuesday in April. I don't know what they are now, or where they are now, but I do know I will never know until the time I am met with that same fate. And *that* scares me half to death (no pun intended).

Death is another one of the great unknowns, a sign of our human fallibility and humility. Every religion has its theory, and each person has his or her own suspicions, but there is just no way of knowing what comes next. And for some of us, that thought is absolutely terrifying. I like to think there is equal chance that everyone's theory is right. I like to think there might be some kind of reincarnated storyline for each of us, like a character out of an Amy Tan book. Or maybe there is a utopian heaven, where there is a calm peace and clarity, reunions with loved ones, bowls of cookie dough, and lots of hugs and dancing. I like to imagine my grandma as a rose garden, my grandpa sitting in a big soft chair smoking his pipe and watching the world go by. I hope that my other grandpa is somewhere enjoying a whiskey on the rocks while he throws dice, laughing loudly and loving the next life as much as he loved this one.

I like to think these things because they make me feel peaceful and happy and a little less scared. But as much as I like to believe in reincarnation, heaven, or some kind of source into which we all return, I also need to acknowledge that there might not be any of these things. We might simply be met with a blank nothingness, a disintegration of body and evaporation of spirit. The only certainty is that the possibilities are infinite and unknown.

A few months ago, while wasting time on Facebook, I came across the following story (the origins of which seem to be unknown):

> *In a mother's womb were two babies. One asked the other, "Do you believe in life after delivery?"*
>
> *The other replied, "Why, of course. There has to be something after delivery. Maybe we are here to prepare ourselves for what we will be later."*
>
> *"Nonsense," said the other. "There is no life after delivery. What would that life be?"*
>
> *"I don't know, but there will be more light than here. Maybe we will walk with our legs and eat from our mouths."*
>
> *The other says, "This is absurd! Walking is impossible. And eat with our mouths? Ridiculous. The umbilical cord supplies nutrition. Life after delivery is to be excluded. The umbilical cord is too short."*
>
> *"I think there is something and maybe it's different than it is here."*
>
> *The other replies, "No one has ever come back from there. Delivery is the end of life, and in the after-delivery it is nothing but darkness and anxiety and it takes us nowhere."*
>
> *"Well, I don't know," says the other, "but certainly we will see Mother and she will take care of us."*
>
> *"Mother? You believe in Mother? Where is she now?"*
>
> *"She is all around us. It is in her that we live. Without her there would not be this world."*

"I don't see her, so it's only logical that she doesn't exist."

To which the other replied, "Sometimes when you're in silence you can hear her, you can perceive her. I believe there is a reality after delivery and we are here to prepare ourselves for that reality."

Could life be preparation for the reality of afterlife? And if so, what does that afterlife consist of? Heaven, reincarnation, legacy, something else entirely? Or could this human life be all we have, our only chance to make good and do good? Could God be the mother voice talking to us in silent and unspeakable sound waves? Or is the mother voice our subconscious brain guiding us on the path? Is there heaven, rebirth, or memory?

I don't know.

Ultimately, though, the answers to these questions don't matter as much as that we keep asking them. What matters is how we choose to use the uncertainty and array of possibilities to live our best life. One of the greatest gifts of humankind is our ability to exercise free will and choose what to believe and how to act. There is no way to know what comes next, but there is choice and there is possibility. There is connection.

I doubt the caterpillar knows what "afterlife" awaits it when it curls up into its cocoon. The only thing it knows is that it's tired, so very tired, and needs to rest. I doubt the caterpillar has any idea that its "next life" consists of brightly colored wings and flying with the birds, just like I doubt the unborn fetus knows that when it leaves the underwater world of its mother's womb, its next life will be one of air-breathing and milk-drinking, one of impossible sadness and unimaginable joys.

While some religions and some religious-types tend to think that their suspicions are the right ones, when it comes to what-comes-next and other great unknowns, there are no wrong beliefs as long as they are grounded in connection rather than division. I make the choice to believe in the possibility of an afterlife (while learning to accept that there may not be one). I choose to believe in an afterlife, whether it's reincarnation or heaven, a world of ghosts or angels, not out of some firm conviction that I am right, but simply because this is the belief that keeps me centered and connected to the world around me. Were it not for a hope in an afterlife, I would be so fearful of leaving the life and people I love that I would crumble into a heap of detachment, leaving just a shell struggling to survive. I choose to believe in a TBD what-comes-next because it keeps me engaged and invested in the world around me. Without hope and faith in the infinite possibility of what-comes-next, this world looks a little less vibrant to me.

Facing my own mortality and the what-comes-next has always been an anxiety-inducing and heart-pounding concept for me. I can tell myself I'm worried about who will take care of the boys, who will get them off to school each morning and make sure their homework is done, and who will show up at their Mother's Day school performances. Or I'm worried about how Matt will manage it all with the immense task of parenting to handle on his own. But the truth is, they would all be just fine. Sure, they would grieve, mourn, and struggle for a while, but together they would cope and learn to manage their new reality. I can tell myself I worry about *them* and all the ways their lives would be worse off without a mother or wife. But I know the greatest loss would be *mine*. I would miss seeing the boys go to prom and learn to drive and get married and have babies. I would miss all of the kissing and singing and dancing. I would miss Matt's laugh and smile and touch. I would miss fresh-baked cookies and summer thunderstorms and tart peaches. The real loss would be *mine,* because there is so much about this life to love and enjoy, and my real fear about death is that what-comes-next just won't be nearly as sweet as this one.

The uncertainty of what-comes-next can be paralyzing at times, pulling us into our shells with false certainty, rules of salvation, and rote religious taglines. It can seal us off with lack of emotional investment or spiritual risk. But when we put those lids of certainty on the mystery of what-comes-next, we miss out on its inherent beauty. The mystery and wonder of what-comes-next is a thousand twinkling lights of possibility that we try to mold into a laser beam of precision. And while the laser beam might seem more practical, more useful, and more reliable, it is the twinkly lights that are more beautiful, more captivating, and more connective.

It is the twinkly lights that glow in the dark corners of uncertainty. And it just might be those twinkly lights that shine the path from this life to what lies on the other side.

Everyday Miracles

"Miracles are a retelling in small letters of the very
same story which is written across the whole world in
letters too large for some of us to see."
—C.S. Lewis

Treadmills and Breast Pumps

"Let us be grateful to people who make us happy,
they are the charming gardeners who make
our souls blossom."
—Marcel Proust

I am an introvert in almost every respect. Crowds of people and attention make me uncomfortable. Not surprisingly, I am apprehensive about meeting new people, and given the choice, I often prefer solitude. So when I do socialize, I will almost always choose the company of a few close friends and intimate conversation to a rousing party filled with acquaintances and small talk. I am empathetic and shy, sometimes debilitating so.

One of the greatest benefits to being an introvert whose easiest connection to the Divine is through personal relationships is that it takes very little to impress me. The most basic gesture of kindness has the ability to bring me to tears, causing my heart to swell to near bursting: A neighbor who lets my dogs out while I am gone for the day. A friend who takes my son to school each morning. A thoughtful and helpful e-mail from a fellow writer— someone I've never met in person—with advice and guidance about the book publishing process. All of these gestures are done without personal agenda for the sole purpose of helping another person, of making someone's load a little lighter.

And like many introverts (and extroverts, for that matter), I value my friendships immensely. In fact, on those days when I'm not even sure if I believe in God, friendship is the living, breathing proof that pulls me through the shadow of doubt. Friendship is a lifeline to the Divine—God on speed dial. One of my favorite writers, Shauna Niequist, says friendship brings the divine into daily life, a way to "remind one another of the bigger, more beautiful picture that we can't always see from where we are."[35] Not only is friendship a divine gift, it's a miraculous discovery. Like finding a bracelet in the couch cushions that we hadn't even known was missing.

I have just a handful of close friends and, unfortunately, time and circumstances have relegated us to various cities across the country. Yet these dear friends are embedded in my heart, like an old and worn pendant I no longer realize is hanging around my neck.

I have known my friend Terra since we were in second grade. We were the last two girls to get picked for just about every gym class activity so, naturally, we became instant friends. It wasn't until college, however, that our friendship really flourished. I'd been struggling with my eating disorder and life as I knew it had shifted on its axis. Pub-crawls and late-night dancing were replaced with long runs and multiple trips to the gym each day. A diet of pizza and beer became microscopic meals at home. I became almost unrecognizable, both physically and emotionally, and lost many friends during that time. I just wasn't that fun or healthy to be around.

But those friendships that did last were transformed. Terra reluctantly ate the awful black-bean brownies that I made. She went on way-too-long bike rides with me. She celebrated my birthday even though it was hardly a gala worthy of attendance. And when I finally admitted I had a problem and needed help, she agreed and helped me recover.

Also during this time, I shared an apartment with my friend Kelly who endured the stench of sweaty sports bras and running shorts around our apartment. There was no judgment, no

---

[35] Niequist, *Cold Tangerines,* 49.

eye rolling, no gossiping. Just a quiet presence and an underlying measure of love and support. Kelly and I had been friends since our freshman year of college. Our rooms were right next door to each other, and after one long and lazy afternoon conversation in October, during which we told brave secrets and laughed until we cried, we knew we had something special. Kelly later became an early-childhood teacher—a great outlet for her voice of reason and compassion—and one of the best mothers I know. So, naturally, whenever I am experiencing those ohmygosh-I-have-no-idea-what-to-do parenting moments, I always ask myself, "What would Kelly do?" and I'm usually guided down the right path.

As I write this, I am sitting at a long dining room table next to my friend Angie, a photographer I met in high school. We are spending the weekend at a friend's bed and breakfast. We got together with the intention of working, keeping each other on task, and tapping into each other's creative energies, but most of our time has been spent talking about everything from children and families to religion and work. In some respects, Angie and I are so similar that we seem like we were cut from the same cloth. We are from the same hometown, and we are both shy, impatient, and opinionated. In other ways, we are starkly different. Angie loves living in Chicago; I am a suburbanite who is a small-town girl at heart. Angie is blonde; I am brunette with the occasional streaks of red or pink or violet. Angie sees life in images; I see life in words. On some issues, we agree passionately; on other issues, we disagree passionately. Voices and emotions might rise, but through it all there is no doubt that the ties of friendship hold it all together despite any differences in opinion or choices or lifestyles.

Throughout the years, these friends and I have seen each other through devastating heartbreak, bitter and jealous arguments, cross-country moves, and countless bad choices. And we have been there for each other's most joyous occasions—marriage, positive pregnancy tests, babies, and job promotions. They are far more than close friends; they are *soul* friends. They are miracles.

Terra lives in Philadelphia now, while I'm still in Chicago, yet we talk via e-mail almost every day, and I see her every couple of months when she comes back to Chicago on business. She stayed with us on a recent visit and, in the wee morning hours, while I sweated and ran on the treadmill, she sat in a chair with a double breast-pump attached to her chest and we talked. We talked and talked and talked. When it became clear that she wasn't going to make the early commuter train into the city like she had planned, I remember thinking, *This is it.* This sharing, this vulnerability, this connecting of one person to another—*this* is what really matters. This is where the sacred lives. This is where the ordinary becomes extraordinary and where the everyday becomes divine. Her words mingled with my words, and amidst stinky sweat and awkward breast pumps, we opened boxes, threw our messes on the floor, and then tied them together as best we could.

I no longer live in the same city as Kelly, Terra, Angie, and we haven't for several years. Yet despite the distance, our friendships continue to grow and thrive and build. And that's a miracle, indeed, especially given the season of life we are in—of babies and job relocations, of never-enough-time and constant exhaustion, of marriage challenges, of falling away and losing touch and Facebook-only communication, of family priorities and job obligations, and friends falling farther down the list.

Perhaps this is also the season during which we need friendship the most. Could this season be the one in which we reconnect with friends who have fallen away, or when we allow ourselves to be vulnerable and open enough to create new friendships? Could this be the season that we'll experience the miracle of friendship?

Then again, maybe it's always the season for the miracle of friendship.

A few days ago I learned of the passing of a good friend's mom. Given that she'd died nearly six month earlier, the news shook me on a number of levels. The death of a peer's parent is always rather unsettling since it forces us to face our own parents' mortality. It reminds us that we are in this delicate middle place where we are both parent and child, but our identity as child could be coming to an end.

When I read the news (via Facebook, of course), I was devastated for my friend, knowing how close she and her mom had been, and I was sad for the world, knowing it was deprived of one of the loveliest women I've known. But on a more personal level, I was confused and sad to realize our friendship was no longer what it once was. *How did this happen?* How did this friend turn into an acquaintance? How did a friendship that had been built on honest communication and truth-telling turn into a relationship that was separate and silent?

How did this person go from a close friend who had come into my room sobbing, begging me to get help for my eating disorder, and was now a relative stranger who didn't want to reach out to me at any point during her mom's year-long battle with uterine cancer or the grieving months after her death?

How did this happen? I wanted to ask. But I knew the answer. It happened because that's what happens with some friendships. They evolve and change, the threads of connection sometimes growing thinner and other times twisting themselves so tightly around each other that it's impossible to tell where one starts and the other ends. I didn't need to ask how this once-strong friendship had fallen into one of disconnected acquaintanceship because I knew the answer: husbands, cross-country moves, the daily demands of young children, and not enough effort.

Caroline Myss writes, "We're not meant to be completely independent, but to give and receive. You cannot increase in self-understanding and well-being and simultaneously remain isolated from humanity. You cannot strive for a healthier, more spiritual life if you keep yourself separate and apart from life around you. The journey of the 'self' also involves the journey of the 'other.'"[36]

And there is no way to experience that "other" without the giving of ourselves, without making the time, putting in the effort, and picking up the phone and calling. Certainly friendships, like all relationships, ebb and flow and some run their course and fade downstream. But they don't always have to.

Friendship can be big and bold and powerful, or it can be mild and indifferent and delicate. Friendship can be transformative and sustaining, or it can be measured and fleeting. Friendship can be resilient and reinvented over and over again, or it can stagnate and fall away like crisp leaves in the fall.

The miracle of friendship is when we choose the bold, powerful, transformative, and resilient path. When we grab hold of the friends we love even if they are on a different branch now. Friendship is treadmills and breast pumps and eating instant mashed potatoes in a stuffy dorm room. Friendship is phone calls in the middle of the night and tough conversations about religion, politics, relationships, and the sticky stuff that leaves us closer rather than farther apart. Friendship is phone calls on a Thursday morning because you heard a song that reminded you of her. Friendship is sweatpants and no makeup, wine in plastic cups while watching *Dirty Dancing* for the millionth time. Friendship is truth-telling, tears, and begging a hurting friend to get the help she needs. Friendship is being the help she needs even if she doesn't realize she needs it yet.

Friendship is a miracle, walking that fuzzy line between the human side of things and the other side—the holy side.

---

[36] Myss, *Invisible Acts of Power*, 7.

White Water Rafting

"The purpose of life is to live it, to taste experience
to the utmost, to reach out eagerly and without fear
for newer and richer experience."
—Eleanor Roosevelt

When I was growing up, our family traveled to California every August. My dad had important customers scattered throughout the state so the trip was a hybrid business trip/family vacation. We would spend a day or two just north of Los Angeles before driving up the coast to Monterey, where we would enjoy a weekend watching the sea lions, wandering the aquarium, and biking along the picturesque seventeen-mile-drive. From Monterey, we would drive to San Francisco for a few more business meetings and lots of clam chowder in sourdough bread bowls.

Depending on Dad's business that year, there might be a few other miscellaneous stops along the way for him to meet with customers—Fresno, San Jose, and San Luis Obispo, for instance—but each year, the trip ended with a long weekend in Reno, where my grandparents would meet us for a weekend of slot machines, horseback riding, and all-you-can-eat buffets.

In addition to the requisite business meetings for my dad, these annual "vacations" involved more time in the car with one's family than should probably be permitted by law. My dad passed the time pointing out scenery along the way in the spirit of Clark W. Griswold. My mom would page through magazines, write postcards, or read whatever paperback novel she picked up in the last hotel's gift shop. My brother would sort through football cards or sports magazines. My sister would sleep or listen to music on her Walkman. And I would read and read and read. Whether the innocent *Babysitter Club* adventures I devoured as a pre-teen or the trashy Danielle Steel novels I moved to later on, I immersed myself in the black-and-white pages of books to pass the time, rarely coming up for air to talk or enjoy the views around me. Each attempt at conversation, each stop to take pictures, was an unwelcome diversion from the adventures playing out on the pages of whatever book I was reading at the time.

Most years, the trip followed a predictable and comfortable routine: swimming in Los Angeles, seafood at Abalonetti's in Monterey, lunch at Fisherman's Wharf in San Francisco, the Circus Circus game room in Reno, and sarsaparilla root beer in Virginia City. Although we were halfway across the country and out of our Midwestern comfort zone, there was a certain ease, and an almost lazy security, to the trip because of its recurring schedule, routine, and venues. As a stubborn and headstrong teenager, I found the trip less of an adventure and more of a nuisance many years. It kept me from my friends and all of the exciting goings-on back home. Adventures were something other people had, not me; adventures were found in the pages of my books, not in the backseat of a sedan on a family trip to California.

All of these business-family trips gave me the opportunity to see some really amazing places—the giant redwoods in Yosemite National Park, the rocky cliffs of Carmel and Monterey, the crystal blue waters of Lake Tahoe—that were, unfortunately, lost on me given my teenage woe-is-me and never-enough attitude. A day trip to Yosemite wasn't enough; I wanted to spend a week camping there. An afternoon on a Lake Tahoe beach wasn't enough; I wanted to ski, swim, and hike. I wanted more than the safety and comfort of my careful and predictable life; I wanted stories and drama and exhilaration. I wanted adventures and excitement, like the dramatic stories playing out in the pages of my books, instead of the life I was living.

Then one year my dad surprised us. With poorly hidden enthusiasm, he announced on our first night in Reno that we would be going white water rafting the next day.

"What?" all four of us exclaimed with disbelief, not the least of which was my mom who was struggling to stifle her annoyance at the unexpected outing.

"Are you sure, Phil? That sounds kind of dangerous," she said.

"It'll be fine," my dad responded with a twinkle in his eye.

My younger brother, Al, a jumpy pre-teen, had a million questions. Carrie, my younger sister, said nothing. But given her athletic and competitive spirit, I was pretty sure she was looking forward to displaying her physical prowess. My mom just shook her head and mumbled something about health insurance and wanting to make it home alive.

I was skeptical. Not about the outing, per se, but more so about its potential to actually be the exciting adventure I was longing for. *It'll probably just be some lazy ride down the river, except I'll actually have to paddle and do something and all for some borrrring ride down the river when we could be doing something FUN and EXCITING, something I could actually tell my friends about instead of some borrrring raft ride down the river.*

The next morning we ate an early breakfast (which wasn't anything out of the ordinary since my dad was always awake, showered, and dressed by seven-thirty, after which he promptly required a bowl of Special K, orange juice, a cup of decaf, and the newspaper) and drove to the Truckee River.

After signing the requisite legal waivers and donning our bright orange life jackets, we waited around for our tour guide to give us the pre-rafting lecture.

Within a few minutes, our tan and toned twenty-something guide called us over, along with the handful of other people who would be riding in our raft.

"Morning, y'all," he drawled out as he introduced himself. "You have chosen the Class 3 rapids, which means you should all be fairly decent swimmers."

He scoped us out, clearly taking internal mental notes on which of us would need the most help if we went overboard.

"There are six classes of rapids so this one is, obviously, right in the middle in terms of difficulty. You will need to paddle. A lot. And you will get wet."

Maybe this won't be just another lazy float down the river, I thought. *But did he say a lot of paddling? And a lot of getting wet? Maybe I'd rather just be back at the hotel reading a book.*

"Most of the ride will be fairly smooth," he said, "but you'll still need to paddle and listen closely to my instructions."

Phew.

"There are a few spots with some pretty big rocks and some fairly strong eddies, however. It's very important that you listen to my instructions and stay calm. When the waters get really rough, I might ask some of you to stop paddling and call out to others to paddle harder so we can steer clear of the rocks. If we do hit a rock, the raft could get stuck, so let's really try to avoid that. Alrighty?

"If you do happen to fall out of the raft," he continued, "stay calm. Lift your legs up to the surface. Even though the water is shallow, you shouldn't try to stand on the bottom since the rocks are sharp and the water moves faster down there. Just lift your feet out of the water, legs straight, and float feet first down the river. One of our rafting experts will throw you a rope and get you back into the raft or onto dry land."

Good Lord, I sure hope nothing like that *happens. I want thrilling, but not dangerous, for goodness sake. And how embarrassing it would be to actually fall out of the raft!*

We loaded the raft, grabbed our oars, and snuggled in with the other family that had been assigned to our raft, and then we were off, floating down the Truckee River. For an hour we paddled and floated, the raft moving quickly but smoothly. After an hour, my arms were pretty sore and the sun was getting hot. I was hungry and thirsty and basically just wanted to be back on dry land. Sufficiently satisfied with the newness of the excursion, I was ready to be done.

"Hang on!" our guide called out. "This final stretch is the choppiest so hold tight to your oars, keep your feet firmly planted in the raft, and listen closely to my commands."

Good grief, I thought, eyeing the rapids just ahead. *Can't we just be done already?*

And that was the last thought that crossed my mind before we hit the large boulder in the middle of the river. It all happened so quickly. One minute I was in the raft, the next minute I was not. I'm sure the guide had yelled some necessary orders I hadn't heard or hadn't obeyed. I was probably daydreaming about what to eat for lunch or some boy back home. I'd probably been lazy and didn't paddle hard enough or lean in the right direction with enough strength. In any event, before I knew it, the raft was stuck and I was in the river.

The rest of the raft's passengers were jostled about a bit too, however. My mom was launched in my direction, landing on top of my feet. So while my entire upper body was completely submerged and held underwater by the suction-cup force of the rapids, my feet were still connected to the raft, held in place by the strength of my mom's hands.

With my head submerged, time slowed considerably, as if to give me time to etch it all in my mind. Through the crystal-clear water, I could see my mom above me, her face a wild mixture of panic, fear, and anger at my dad's hair-brained idea to subject us to this excursion.

Behind my mom, I saw a pale blue sky framed by the lush and rugged hills of the Sierra Nevada Mountains. I heard the roar of the rapids and saw my mom screaming, "Get her out! Get her out!" I felt her knees and hands firmly planted on my feet. And I laughed.

Smiling and laughing, I didn't want it to end. I wanted to stay submerged in this somewhat dangerous position, with its unique and unforgettable perspective, while knowing I was connected safely (albeit somewhat tenuously) to the raft as long as possible.

Just as quickly as I had been thrown out of the raft, our guide heaved me back into the raft and it was over. We were stuck on a rock in the middle of the river so we had a few moments for us all to catch our breath. My mom was still a little frantic, though somewhat calmer now that my entire body was in the raft instead of just my feet. My brother and sister were trying not to laugh, and my dad had this odd look of pride on his face. The other family just sat motionless, the parents smugly pleased that one of their children hadn't fallen out of the raft.

Within a few minutes, the guide on another raft threw us a rope to pull us down from the boulder and shortly thereafter we arrived ashore, without further incident. I dried off and reassured my mom that I was fine.

"Are you sure you're okay? Did you hit your head?" she kept asking.

"I'm fine," I said dismissively though I knew, without a doubt, that I was most assuredly *not* fine.

I was *more* than fine. I felt exhilarated, amazing, wholly and completely alive. I had experienced my first great adventure, after all.

In those all-too-brief moments when the rapids sang in my ears, the water washed over my face, the skies sparkled above me, and the mountains hugged it all in close, I experienced the thrill of adventure with the safety of connection. And isn't that what we're all secretly striving for? Aren't we all looking for a way to feel the intoxication of adventure and the excitement of new experiences without all the risks and discomforts that come along with it?

Sometimes the risks are too high; other times, the adventure seems illusive. Whatever the reason, we tuck ourselves into our routines and our comfort zones. We shy away from new experiences and difficult tasks, turning to what we know and what carries the least discomfort. We live vicariously through others, whether the globe-trotting friend, the colleague who brazenly asks for a raise, or some character in one of our novels. Adventures are for other people, we tell ourselves, even as we lament our predictable and innocuous lifestyle.

I had assumed that adventure and excitement and daring were these BIG and BOLD things other people did. Adventures were not for me, as much as I craved them in theory. Adventures looked good on paper; in practice, not so much. And, what's more, it's not like adventures were knocking down my door. It isn't that easy, after all, to have BIG and BOLD adventures living in a small town in Wisconsin. Or a large suburb of Chicago, for that matter.

I'm not meant to live a life of adventure, I rationalized. *I'm meant to live a life of stability and security and safety.*

All too often, I have told myself that I wanted adventure and excitement, thrills and exhilaration, and then when push came to shove, I turned away from it. In many instances, I have taken the safe route or chosen the most comfortable option, and then lamented my innocent and unexciting life. Adventures, I'd thought, were these lofty expeditions best left for other people, for braver people. But if I learned anything from that white water rafting tour, it is this: First, adventure is everywhere an adventurous spirit endures and, second, the risks of adventure can always be managed if we stay connected to someone or something.

Adventure isn't just found in far-off exotic locations or death-defying feats, though it certainly can be. Adventure is found anytime we step out of our comfort zone, look at things from a different perspective, and approach a new experience with a daring spirit and an open mind. Taking a cooking class, learning a new language, watching a foreign film. Visiting a new park, driving home via a different route, climbing a tree in the backyard. Inviting a new friend to coffee, dancing in public, running a 5K.

Adventure isn't *out there*; adventure is *in here*, in and around each one of us. There are risks and dangers and discomfort, but as long as we have faith that someone or something—whether God or the Spirit, the support of family or the love of friends, personal strength or fierce resiliency—we will always be connected to the raft.

With that safety line connecting us together, we can see things we never imagined and know a lightness of spirit we never thought possible.

Bugs and Other Such Ugliness

"Beauty is unbearable, drives us to despair,
offering us for a minute the glimpse of an eternity
that we should like to stretch out over the
whole of time."
—Albert Camus

I have a confession to make. I am a recovering bug murderer.

Until a few years ago, I had no problem squishing spiders, swatting flies, and crushing unknown miscellaneous creepy-crawlies. All of that changed, however, when my oldest son developed an obsession with animals shortly after he was born. Jackson is fascinated with all of God's creatures, from majestic elephants and fierce lions to slithering snakes and spindly spiders. So much so that, upon seeing a colony of ants that had taken up residence on our kitchen counter, he reprimanded me for using an eco-friendly pest spray because "it might kill the ants." I couldn't bring myself to tell him that that was the point.

My son's passion has forced me to see these nasty pests in a whole new light. Well, most of the time, anyway.

Upon seeing a big, nasty, disgusting bug on my kitchen floor, I wouldn't hesitate to step on it, crush it, and flush it down the toilet. But now I'm able to see that same bug just a little differently. Under the filtered afternoon sunlight, it is still just as big, nasty, and disgusting, but now I notice its tiny moving limbs and admire it for what it really is—a life-giving, life-sustaining, indispensable participant in the vitality of nature. It's a tiny miracle, whether it's shimmering in the sunlight or scuttling into dark corners of the kitchen. So now, instead of instinctively crushing that nasty little bugger, I look the other way, or I call my son and ask him to set it free for me.

Just like our impressions of bugs on our kitchen floor can change, so too can our impressions of bugs in our lives change depending on the framework we provide for them. We can see a challenging, painful, or stressful experience as a horribly unfair, no-win situation. Or we can see the circumstances for what they truly are.

Of course, bad things happen. Terrible, unjust, awful, ghastly, no-good-reason, bad things happen. And we have every right to be sad, to mourn, to grieve, to be pissed off, and to wail, "Why me?"

But once we step back from the pain of the situation and gain some perspective, grace shines a light and we can see the situation for what it is. A nasty, ugly, creepy-crawly, and kind of *beautiful* bug.

When I became pregnant with my oldest son, like most first-time expectant parents I was filled with optimism and promise. We told our family about the pregnancy shortly after the double pink lines appeared on the stick, before I had even been to the doctor to confirm the pregnancy.

Two weeks later and a few days before my first ultrasound was scheduled, we met some friends in Arizona for a long weekend of baseball games, lounging by the pool, and wine-soaked dinners (or, in my case, club soda-soaked dinners). At some point during that weekend, I became utterly convinced that I was having a miscarriage. I didn't have morning sickness. My breasts weren't tender. I didn't feel exhausted. I was certain I wasn't actually pregnant and I became paralyzed with fear that we would be calling our family back home to tell them that it was, indeed, a false alarm. There was no baby.

Well, despite my fears, there was a baby, a tiny little pea we saw on the ultrasound the following Monday. The rest of that pregnancy was relatively comfortable and predictable.

Two years later, I found myself holding another stick with two pink lines on it. Startled and pleasantly surprised, I made the necessary doctor appointments, but afraid that I might set off a cosmic firestorm if we shared our news too quickly, we kept it to ourselves. A week later, I experienced my first miscarriage. It was an early miscarriage, with little drama, except for the sharp disappointment and dull emptiness that remained.

Because we hadn't told anyone about the pregnancy, we didn't need to tell anyone about the loss either. So no one asked, no one called, no one cried with me. Of course, I shouldn't have expected consolation since we hadn't told anyone I was pregnant in the first place, and on the rare occasion we did tell someone about the early miscarriage, my husband and I often downplayed the experience, passing it off as "no big deal."

Just three months later, I found myself pregnant again. Given the previous miscarriage, Matt and I were timid with our excitement and anticipation. Yet with each doctors' appointment and each day that went by, we grew more and more optimistic. I was sick this time, on more than one occasion finding myself doubled over with nausea while walking the dogs around the block. And I was exhausted. Not just tired, but uncontrollably and incomprehensibly exhausted. The sickness, the exhaustion, and the blood test results built my hopes and visions of this new baby. I could even see her—a girl, I was certain of it. My due date was Christmas Day. Maybe we would name her Eve.

When I was eight weeks pregnant, however, the baby's heartbeat was barely recognizable.

"You are miscarrying," the doctor said.

"But I'm not bleeding! I have morning sickness! I'm exhausted!" I told them. "I must be pregnant."

"Schedule a D&C," she said.

"Okay," I sighed.

So the following Monday, my mom at home with Jackson, Matt and I drove to the hospital. I walked in with a heavy heart and a dead baby inside me; I walked out with an empty womb and an empty soul. I spent the day sleeping and resting, eating when I could. But I don't think I shed a single tear that day.

Over the next few months, I distracted myself with various social plans and caring for Jackson, who, like most almost-two-year-old boys, was a flurry of excitement and mischief. Matt was consumed with work obligations and career stress. This was the summer of 2008, so there was a constant haze of financial uncertainty that cast a pall over our career choices, lifestyle, and future.

I hid my pain in these everyday distractions, using them like a bristly blanket to smother the flames of anger and bitterness smoldering inside. I was angry at just about everyone and everything. Angry that they didn't ask how I was doing, that they didn't know this kind of pain, and that they were still carrying on with their lives as if the world was still spinning as normal when mine had come to a screeching halt.

When I did shed tears, I shed them alone. Matt and I rarely talked about the loss, the pain, and the uncertainty, except in hushed whispers under the cover of still darkness. Few people asked, and we didn't share. Because, really, how could I have explained that the doctor had cut out a tiny piece of my soul when he used his cold metal tools?

I tried to minimize the pain, but its impact simmered below the surface and bubbled up in odd and misplaced ways. It was months before I could bring myself to hold my niece, who was born just days after our baby had been due to be born. An elusive hopelessness settled in, along with an unpredictable bitterness and a resigned loss of faith, which manifested itself in misplaced and misdirected ways.

The pain and sadness of those miscarriages eventually led to the confusion and desperation of continued fertility struggles, including another early miscarriage. I saw doctors and specialists, I took tests and medications, and I had surgeries and was probed more often and in more ways than I care to remember.

Over the next year or so, my life fell into a kind of holding pattern like one of the airplanes that line the runways at Chicago's O'Hare airport. I was waiting for the signal that my life could take off, that I could leave this perpetual cycle of ovulation tests and blood draws and dashed hopes.

Then one day in early June of 2009, there were two lines on the stick. I took another test just to be sure. Two lines. I took another test just to be *really* sure. Two lines. I frantically rushed to the fertility clinic (the nurses knew my son and me by name at this point) for a pregnancy test before heading out of town for a couple of days to visit my family in Wisconsin.

The next morning, waking up early in my parents' house, I took another test and there were no double pink lines. Just one lonely line. I took another test. One line. I took another one and another one and another one. All one line. I let the tears fall, fast and furious. They fell with hiccups and angry fists. They fell with cries of "why me?" and "it's not fair!" They fell with helplessness, confusion, and anger. Since I was visiting my parents for a few days, I snuggled into the safe cocoon of home and family. I wept with my sister and vented to my mom. And then I read books with my son and thanked God that he was healthy and happy, surrounded by people who loved him to the moon and back.

I felt the familiar waves of sorrow and I grieved, again.

Two days later, the doctor called. I was, surprisingly, pregnant. Or at least I had been two days ago when the blood tests were taken. More tests were needed to determine whether I was still pregnant, which, of course, I was not. The pink-line tests said so.

Except it turns out that I was still pregnant. This little miracle baby, who I was certain was not meant to be, was still there. A few weeks later, we saw the tiny and quick little heartbeat. And as I described in the "Star Stuff" chapter, when we finally heard that *whoosh-whoosh-whoosh* of life at my twelve-week appointment, I lay on the table and sobbed. I sobbed, desperately and uncontrollably. I cried for all of the unshed tears of the previous miscarriages. I cried for all of the physical pain and the unspeakable emotional pain we had endured over the past two years. I cried for the lost babies, the vanishing heartbeats, the countless visits to the fertility clinic, the surgeries, the needles, the tests, and the emotional rollercoaster, the unstable hormones, the false hopes and the shattered dreams. But I also cried for the unwavering faith that somehow, some way we would survive. I cried for the miracle of life, for this Spirit-infused soul who a few weeks ago had been as big as a cocooned caterpillar and was now the size of a butterfly. And five months later, this little miracle baby, Theodore, came into the world and our family.

In *Bittersweet*, Shauna Niequist writes of her miscarriages this way[37]:

> *It's easy to believe that having a child is as simple as growing tomatoes: you do the right couple things, you take your prenatals and avoid caffeine and nitrates, and the universe hands you a perfect life, right on schedule. But if you've ever tried growing anything—a tomato plant, a baby, anything—you know it's more mysterious and more treacherous than that . . . There's a mystery we tend not to acknowledge until certainty has been ripped out of our*

---

[37] Shauna Niequist, *Bittersweet*, (Grand Rapids: Zondervan, 2010), 44.

*clutching hands. And only when certainty is gone do we
allow ourselves to bend and open to that terrifying mystery,
dark and incomprehensible.*

I don't know about you, but I have the hardest time
growing tomatoes; growing babies proved to be equally as difficult.

And without the baby I so desperately wanted—without
my tomato, so to speak—all I could see were the nasty bugs
crawling on me and in me. The bugs were the enemy, threatening
to creep into my life to destroy my plans and prevent my
happiness. I tried to pretend the bugs weren't there, but that only
made them grow bigger and look scarier.

Now, years later and with my two boys asleep in their
beds, I can see this situation for what it was and I can see the bugs
for what they were and are. Yes, the situation was horrible,
devastating, and painful in ways I never could have predicted. And
yes, the bugs—the fear, doubt, and loss—were unpleasant to deal
with and pretty scary sometimes. But with their beady eyes and
smooth skin, they were also kind of beautiful in a raw and
illuminating way. I used to think of bugs as unpleasant nuisances,
lacking any redeeming qualities, something to be rid of as quickly as
possible. But slowly over the past few years, I am realizing that
bugs, whether on the ground or in our hearts, aren't just nasty and
disgusting nuisances. They are regenerators, rejuvenators, evolvers,
and an intricate part of life's web.

Let me be clear: I don't believe in a God who tests us to
see what we can handle, nor do I believe in a vengeful God. I don't
believe that the universe operates on a *quid pro quo* basis, or that
there is some cosmic purpose or fate-driven reason for life's
disasters. And while I am generally incredibly optimistic, sometimes
there are clouds that just do not have a silver lining.

But if you believe in God—and most days I do—you keep
looking for the silver lining, keep searching for the beauty in the
bug, keep holding on to the relentless and unwavering potential of

love even amidst all of the hate. "Composting for the soul," Niequist calls it, using the "smashed up garbage to bring about something new and good, however tiny."[38]

All around us there is incomprehensible devastation pushing us to scream, "Why? Why? Why?" The Newtown school massacre, the Boston marathon bombing, and 9/11. Car accidents, medical conditions, and untimely deaths. There is a natural tendency to respond to the devastation with anger. Some people question humanity or God. Others demand justice for the tragedies, calling for retribution and retaliation.

But others—fewer, but still many—respond with courage, bravery, empathy, and forgiveness, knowing that only by acting with love, compassion, and resiliency can we ever truly be saved from fear and win the fight. They know that amidst the blood and horror and ugliness—not just in Boston and Newtown, but in the world as a whole—there is a hidden beauty around us, among us, and within us.

There is bravery evidenced by those who run in to help when human instinct is to run out. Joy shines through the faces of smiling children. Passion is felt in the embrace of ecstatic lovers. Compassion spills forth from hearts all over who ache for the hurt and weary. Resiliency is demonstrated by the determination of everyone willing to get back up after they fall. Rebirth sprouts from the buds that begin to peek through the cold, sodden ground of early spring.

Yes, there is cruelty, death, chaos, confusion, devastation, ugliness, and misery. There always has been; there always will be. And sometimes, because it is loud, brash, and obnoxious, the ugliness is just so obvious. But if you look closely—really closely—

---

[38] Niequist, *Bittersweet*, 121.

you can see that the beauty is bigger, stronger, and greater than the ugliness ever could be.

By seeing the hidden beauty, we can work to eradicate the ugliness. By facing our fears, we can take the first cautious steps toward feeling safe. By loving fully and completely, with a whole and open heart, we can feel the gentle hand of grace.

The ugliness, the devastation, and the bugs of life have a way of getting at us and getting into us, making us feel scared and unsafe and utterly grossed out. But put those bugs on a dazzling flower and they can almost—*just almost*—become beautiful. I wouldn't wish the fertility problems and miscarriages that Matt and I suffered on anyone, but I can tell you that when those gnarled bugs were surrounded by the petals of resilience and renewed appreciation for each other and Jackson, well, they started to look just a little bit less gnarled. Still ugly and kind of gross, yes, but not quite so scary.

When we are able to see the beauty in all the ugliness, when we are able to see things for what they are and not for what we wanted them to be or what they might have been, then we are fortunate to be one of the lucky ones who can see the beauty in the ugliness.

There are bugs, some nasty and scary, others glossy and kind of pretty. There are disasters and there are miracles. There are caterpillars and there are butterflies. Always, there is beauty. The miracle is finding it.

We are opening boxes, sorting through what is inside. We are searching and we are finding. We are tying threads. We are connecting the pieces.

Dance Lessons

"I would believe only in a God that knows
how to dance."
—Friedrich Nietzsche

Matt and I were married ten years ago on a warm April
afternoon. The wedding, by most accounts, was a traditional and
relatively modest affair. We were married in my hometown, a small
rural farming community in central Wisconsin, by a Lutheran
minister who was a close friend of the family. My parents hosted a
post-nuptial happy hour in their backyard, and the reception
continued at the Hilton Garden Inn just off the highway. There
was no entourage of stylists, hairdressers, or makeup artists. My
best friend's mom did my hair. My dad cooked us eggs the
morning of the wedding, and I lounged on my parents' living room
couch with my dress—a traditional princess gown from House of
Brides—splayed around me.

One of our few wedding splurges: dance lessons.

Eager to break with tradition in some fashion and avoid
the same old wedding dance (swaying back and forth in the middle
of the dance floor while guests drained champagne glasses and
munched on crudités), we bought a package of private dance
lessons at a studio near my apartment in downtown Chicago. For
three months, we met on Wednesday evenings with a dance
instructor, practicing the foxtrot and the waltz, two of the easiest
and most beginner ballroom dances.

On our wedding day, while Etta James belted out "At
Last," Matt and I sashayed across the dance floor moving with our
rehearsed steps, spins, and twirls and concluding with a long and

low dip, to which the wedding guests went wild. Even now when I watch the wedding video, I can honestly say that despite the hefty price tag, the dance lessons paid off.

Yet even though that first dance at our wedding reception was a resounding success, it doesn't come close to topping the list of my best dances. I have danced many dances, each one of them sacred in its own way, each one a manifestation of the Divine, and each one a miracle.

When Jackson was just an infant, I was consumed by raging hormones and fear. Most days, I wasn't sure if or how we would make it through the day. When one of us wasn't crying, he just stared at me with his round, brown eyes with a look that seemed to say, "Well, what are we going to do now?" To which I wanted to say, "How about we both take a nice long nap and then I'll have a cup of coffee while I read the newspaper and you page through *Green Eggs and Ham?*" Jackson didn't much care for that plan so we did the next best thing—we danced. Every afternoon I would choose some music from my favorite playlist, which at the time included a lot of melancholy folksy music, and we would dance together in our small family room. His tiny head could not yet support its own weight, so he rested on my shoulder as we danced a slow and desperate dance, sheltering ourselves from the chaotic confusion of these new lives of ours.

With the late afternoon darkness of winter descending outside, these dances freed us. I don't think I am being dramatic when I say that these dances saved us as well. While some parents might remember rocking their newborns in a plush recliner, snuggling their babies while nursing, watching their eyelids close to sleep, taking long walks with a brand-new stroller, or driving around the block late at night to stop the colicky cries, I will remember these late afternoon dances. Each one a tiny little miracle because they saved us, and they connected us.

I am lucky to have married that rare breed of man who loves to dance, as well. There are a number of reasons why I think

I married well, not the least of which is the fact that Matt likes to dance and is actually good at it. He is always up for dancing, whether in a bar late at night, at a wedding, or in the kitchen on a Friday night, and I hope I'm not pushing my luck by praying that Jackson and Teddy inherit his dancing abilities along with his selflessness, happy heart, and boyish good looks. Because if there is one piece of wisdom I could pass on to my boys, it would be to always dance. Okay, so I would first want to teach them to be brave and kind and loving and joyful, but after all of that I would teach them to always dance.

I love to watch their little bodies move in random, spastic movements, simply because the music moved through them. At some point, I fear that the inhibitions will kick in. They will start to worry about how they look and what others think. But I want to tell them and write it in permanent marker across their hearts: *Don't stop dancing.*

Dance, I will tell them, *always dance*. Don't stand against the wall trying to look cool. Dance. Dance at weddings and in bars and in the car. Dance standing up and sitting down. Dance with your hands, fingers snapping. Dance with your feet, toes tapping. Dance.

Dance. Because nothing looks sexier or more attractive or more fun than someone who dances. Dance with girls and dance with boys. Dance alone and together and in groups. Dance slowly and quickly; dance in whatever speed you feel like dancing. Dance with music and in the quiet. Dance, not just the coordinated dances of ballrooms, but the spirited dances of the soul.

Dance, I will tell them. *Dance*, I will show them. Dance when you're full of energy, and dance when you're exhausted. Dance because you are happy. Dance because you're sad.

Dance to feel the expanse of emotion, to love completely and vividly. Dance in forgiveness and with mercy. Dance with peaceful elegance and with innocent gauche. Dance to break free from restrictions and limitations; dance because sometimes that's all there's left to do. Dance to the music in your soul. Dance to live, to move, to feel. Dance to connect.

Dance with friends and strangers and family. Dance clumsy little jigs of joy and don't worry about the rhythm or tempo or beat. Dance rocking requiems, with tears flowing. Dance with your eyes closed, head swaying, shoulders bobbing, foot tapping. Dance.

Dance, always dance, I will tell them.

Dancing connects people and bodies. It connects the musical with the physical, the sacred with the secular. Dancing closes the gaps, and connects races and genders and classes. Dancing speaks the unspeakable, and understands the inexplicable. Dancing frees us and it saves us; it builds bridges and tears down walls.

Because when we dance, arms whirling and feet bouncing, we're pulling the strands over, under, and through. We've tying strings and weaving threads.

Manna from Heaven

"Nothing would be more tiresome than eating and
drinking if God had not made them a pleasure as
well as a necessity."
—Voltaire

Most experienced gardeners will give you the same advice
on starting a vegetable garden: plant tomatoes. To the experienced
gardener, tomatoes are as sure a crop as there is. Of course, that is
assuming that they get the right amount of sun and water, they are
protected from greedy rabbits and squirrels, and safe from naughty
dogs who like to sneak into the garden and trample the hard-
earned fruits of your labor. For our family, at least one of the
aforementioned requirements seems to be a problem each and
every year. If it's not too hot, there is too little water; if it's not the
rabbits, it's our gluttonous dog. So from one novice gardener to
another, here is my recommendation: plant mint. It is very
forgiving, it grows like a weed, and even if your dog eats it, well, at
least he'll have good breath.

Few things make a person appreciate the miracle of food
quite like attempts to grow one's own, whether it's successful, or
thwarted by poor weather conditions or ill-behaved dogs. I haven't
always had an easy relationship with food. As a child with the
metabolism of an Energizer bunny, I subsisted on salami
sandwiches, potato chips, French onion dip, Twix candy bars, and
copious amounts of Mountain Dew. Until later, in college, I
realized that perhaps my diet should include a few more vegetables
and a little less trans fats.

After gaining far more than the "freshman fifteen," my love for food turned into a fear of food. Where food had once been a source of pleasure, it soon became the source of angst, anxiety, and guilt. Food became less a source of energy or pleasure and more of a number, with calories to be counted and fat content to be minimized. Food lost most of its comfort and enjoyment, let alone any sense of sanctity or connection.

Slowly, over time and with a lot of love and patience, I recovered from that eating disorder I described earlier in "Star Stuff." While I will admit that I don't exactly have a carefree relationship with food, and there are times when I feel myself slipping back into old habits and tendencies, it's generally the run-of-the-mill admonishments about eating a few too many Reese's peanut butter cups or not eating enough kale.

Sometimes, I think, it takes a complete breakdown of sorts, a total separation from what we once knew, to realize the delicate miracle that once was. Whether a friendship fades away, we lose a job that we loved, or we can no longer enjoy a plate of spaghetti, when everything that was good and true and familiar is lost, it's only then that we can see the miracle we had held in our hands. When we're left feeling our way around a dark and toxic tunnel of fear, uncertainty, and shame, we can begin finding our way back to that miracle.

For so many years I took food for granted. My parents made sure there were three square meals on the table each day and plenty of snacks filling our cupboards. I ate when I was hungry, stopped when I was full, and didn't give much thought to where the food came from, why I was eating it, or how it made me feel. Food was just there, and always would be there, like the sun rose in the morning and set in the evening. Food filled a void—a delicious little "hug" or "backrub" when I was scared or worried or stressed. And then food became the enemy, this bully that kept pressuring me and criticizing me, calling me names and berating me like a little devil sitting on my shoulder.

But I am learning to love food again, to honor it and celebrate it. The funny thing is, the more I pay attention and the more I notice, the more I'm able to enjoy and appreciate food. When I stop looking at grocery shopping as this annoying chore on my to-do list, when I think about where my food comes from and the efforts it took to grow it, when I'm mindful of what I eat and how it makes me feel, when I use dinner preparation as a way of sharing love and sustenance, when I thank the sun, the soil, the animals, the plants, and the universe for all that it is, does, and provides, it is *then* that I am able to step into the light and celebrate the absolute miracle of food.

Even at its most basic level, food isn't just a way to fill our bellies but a means of connecting. Food connects our spirit to our body through cravings; it connects our body to all of the plants and animals, the earth and sky, and the rocks and soil that create the things we call food. It connects families and friends and strangers, an expression of love and affection; it connects hearts and minds, opening lines of communication and dialogue. Food connects us to our own soul through the grace of mindfulness as we chop garlic, peel potatoes, and stir risotto. And it connects us to the Divine, as an earthly manifestation of the interconnectedness of all that is.

The smells and tastes of food have a way of stirring up a strange stew of memories and feelings, many of which are so subtle or so ingrained that we might not even notice or acknowledge them. Apple dumplings remind me of my grandma. Corn on the cob tastes like summer. Brats and beer smell like a football tailgate party. Chocolate chip cookies, straight from the oven all warm and gooey, taste a lot like love.

We can't separate the emotions, memories, and feelings that food conjures up, nor do I think we should. Instead, I think it all boils down to mindfulness. Paying attention to what we are eating, where it came from, and the work that went into bringing it to our mouths. Being aware of how food makes us feel and all of the connections—physical, natural, emotional, and spiritual—that food facilitates. And when we are mindful, when we are paying attention and are aware of our food instead of fearing it or taking it for granted, we are better able to appreciate the miracle of it.

Food is associated with a number of deep-seated emotions—nostalgia and comfort, ideas about health and well-being, even feelings of shame and guilt. So many of us try to connect with others or ourselves through food. We show our love through plates of spaghetti and chocolate cake. Or we satisfy an emotional hunger with Kit Kats and bowls of Ben & Jerry's. We bond with friends over burgers, fries, and pitchers of beer.

Nowadays, it seems that everyone has some kind of food restriction or aversion, which can be confusing as all get-out. There is nut-free, gluten-free, and fat-free. Organic, all-natural, non-GMO. The paleo diet, the Mediterranean diet, the Atkin's diet. Vegan, vegetarian, and pescatarian. A few years ago, I became a vegetarian, something that my meat-loving Midwestern family finds utterly perplexing. Until recently, whenever the subject would come up and I reminded my parents that I was vegetarian, my mom would ask, "But you eat chicken, right?" My parents didn't know what to make of the fact that I don't eat meat ("How can you get the nutrients you need?" or "Where's your protein? You need protein!" or "I made some chicken; you eat chicken, right?")

It was unsettling and foreign to my parents that I didn't eat steak or burgers or bacon (or chicken, for that matter). Certain connections had always been made over meals. My dad was a self-professed grill master; my mom a meat-potato-vegetable kind of cook. How would we connect if we weren't enjoying a beef tenderloin fresh off the grill or pork lo mein from the Chinese restaurant in town?

Food also seems to have this strange ability to call our own choices into question. If a friend eats organic produce and whole grains, shying away from sugar and processed foods, what does that say about our own choices to feed our children dinosaur-shaped frozen chicken nuggets and Chef Boyardee? If a family member goes gluten-free, how are we supposed to show our love through our famous banana bread? If a co-worker is vegan, how can we comfortably eat a salami and cheese sandwich in the company cafeteria?

Again, I think it comes back to mindfulness—a mindful awareness of why we are making the food choices that we are making, and a mindful respect for the food choices of others. It takes an awareness of the emotions and attachments that lie buried within our ideas about food and nutrition, love and sustenance. And a little bit of flexibility and tolerance go a long way as well.

A few weeks ago, while at the first football tailgate party of the year—a family ritual that holds a lot of long-standing customs and deep-seated food traditions, not the least of which is a smorgasbord of grilled meats—my dad threw on a few Morningstar black bean burgers for me. Though my dad has nearly fifty years of experience as a tailgating expert, a veggie burger had yet to make its way onto his grill, and he is not one to ask for grilling advice. Nonetheless, I overheard him sheepishly ask my mom, "How do I cook this?"

I don't think I need to tell you that it was one of the best burgers of my life, veggie or otherwise.

When we pay attention to where our food is coming from, its importance in our life, and the attitudes and feelings that are baked into each morsel, then we can connect with our bodies, families, communities, and the earth on a wider and deeper level. We are nourished in a way that food, as nutrients and calories alone, cannot do.

A few months ago, I spent the weekend at a friend's bed and breakfast in the Illinois countryside in the hopes that the seclusion and change of scenery would give me the time, space, and clarity I needed to write. I got very little writing done that weekend. I did, however, do a fair amount of eating and connecting that weekend, and I am profoundly grateful for it.

At night, with the table covered in bottles of wine, loaves of bread, and platters of cheese, we ate and we drank. We laughed and we cried. We talked and we connected.

That night I should have been working, writing some of the essays for this very book. It was, after all, what I had come there to do. Instead, I sat around a table surrounded by women whom I enjoy and admire, eating salty cheese and squishy bread and fudgy brownies. Maybe that's what I had *really* come there to do: eat, bond, and *feel*. Because the food that night, simple and pure, may as well have been manna sent straight from heaven, filling a hunger and feeding a need, creating memories and making miracles.

Valentine's Day

"You are the closest I will ever come to magic."
—Suzanne Finnamore

A letter to my firstborn:

Dear Jackson,

Do you have any idea that you just gave me the very best Valentine's Day present? What you gave me is better than any jewelry, chocolates, or homemade heart-shaped craft project I suspect you will make me in preschool one day. It's better than Hallmark cards and poetry and love songs.

I'll be honest, honey: All those years ago when your daddy and I were falling in love, when all those fleeting images of our would-be family started flashing through my head, I never imaged it would look like this. I envisioned cherub faces and toothless smiles. I dreamed of reading stories together, singing songs, and coloring pictures.

What I didn't imagine was the level of confusion and struggle this whole family-making thing would entail. Sure, I knew there would be sleepless nights, but I always imagined them with the thrill of an all-night study session or in a wild party kind of way, not the painful kick-in-the-stomach it really was.

I never imagined the helplessness that would consume me when I didn't know how to get you to stop crying, or why you had a weird rash on your belly, or why you wouldn't *just go to sleep already*! I never imagined the Groundhog Day-like desperation that would grab hold of my mind, convincing me this was not just a phase, that something was terribly wrong, that we would be stuck in this endless cycle of crying-and-not-sleeping for months, maybe even years.

I imagined I would be seized by love at first sight and a wise mother's instinct. I never imagined that I would fall victim to a paralyzing syndrome of second-guessing and indecision. I had never imagined that ideas and strategies that seemed genius during the day would be completely ridiculous at two o'clock in the morning. And three o'clock. And then again at five o'clock.

I just want to do what is best for you and your daddy and our family. Because, honestly, there is absolutely nothing more important to me than being your mommy and your daddy's wife. And I know I have lost myself a bit in the process, I know I have fallen into this dark hole of emptiness, pushed under by the swirling waves of sadness and loneliness. But I am fighting to get back out. Every day I am clawing my way to the surface, getting a little closer to the light. Every day, I am getting a little closer to you, my sweet boy.

"Enjoy it; it goes so fast," they say.

"It's just a phase; it'll pass," they sigh pitifully.

I've wanted to scream at them. Why do people say these things?

But then last night, when you slept your sweet little dreamless baby sleep for a whole entire night, I realized that they say these things because they are true. It *does* go fast. It *is* just a phase. It *will* pass.

You will be four months old in a few days and already you are like a different baby. You are growing and changing right before my eyes. Sometimes it seems like things will never change and, other times, I look at you and hardly recognize you as the baby I knew the day before. I am growing and changing as well. I am working to heal and rebuild what has been broken so I can love you in the very best way I can.

Your daddy and I are growing and changing too, both individually and together. We are learning how to balance these new roles of Daddy and Mommy with that of Husband and Wife. We are learning the value of communication, appreciation, and mercy. We are learning how to ask for what we need and say "thank you" more often. We are learning and loving just as I hope you will one day with your spouse.

And if there is one thing I could tell you today on your first Valentine's Day, I would tell you that very thing that has made me want to scream and cry more than once in the past four months: Enjoy it; it goes so fast. Enjoy life—all of it—because it really does go so very fast. Some days will seem like time is standing still, like you will never get off the treadmill of sleepless nights and desperate worry and debilitating pain. On some days, you will be convinced you are doing it wrong, that everyone else has all the answers, and you missed that day in school when the Guide to Life's Happiness was handed out. Some days will almost break you, and you'll feel like you cannot possibly make it another day.

But always know that it won't break you and you can make it. You have a light that is stronger than the dark, a spirit that is stronger than the struggle. You will always have Daddy and me on your team. We would fight pirates and lions and villains to keep you safe and happy.

And never forget that, as they say, this too shall pass. Just when you think you can't make it through another day, your almost-four-month-old baby will sleep through the night and give you a Valentine's Day gift of deliciously dreamy slumber. And it is then that you will become painfully aware of just how right they are—that it *will* pass, that it *does* go fast—and you will wish with all your heart, for once, that they were wrong, that it wouldn't go so fast, and that it would stay this way just a little while longer.

Jackson, my sweet boy, I have no idea what the future brings for you. I have no idea what kind of person you will grow into, whether you will like trucks or animals or pirates, whether you will be shy or outgoing, funny or serious. I don't know whether you will be a lawyer or a plumber or a veterinarian or a salesman. I don't know whether you will be a feisty headstrong toddler, a laidback preschooler, or an angry teenager. I don't know if we will fight over car keys or prom dates or poor test scores. I don't know whether you will be on the basketball team or the drama club or the debate team. I don't know if you will move far away one day or whether you will stay close to home.

What I do know is that whatever your future holds, and whatever spinning swirl of life is going on around you and our family, you will be loved completely and unconditionally. And I also know that this morning, this cold Valentine's Day morning, feels like an absolute miracle. All because of you.

Love,
Mommy

Lost and Found

"Childhood is not from birth to a certain age and at
a certain age. The child is grown, and puts away
childish things. Childhood is the kingdom
where nobody dies."
—Edna St. Vincent Millay

Some people lose their car keys, others their reading glasses. I, myself, am perpetually misplacing my favorite lipstick and sunglasses, never sure whether they are in the car, at the bottom of my purse, on the kitchen counter, or left behind somewhere never to be recovered. My husband seems to always be looking for his phone charger; my children, their blankies.

If you are a parent, you can probably understand the attachment that a blankie, a teddy bear, or lovey can bring to a child. Jackson has slept with his blankie for the past 2,555 days (but who's counting) without a night or naptime apart. Shortly after we realized the attachment had formed between Jackson and Blankie (yes, it is a proper noun around our house), we quickly ordered a duplicate on the advice of many parents who had learned the hard way about lost and unrecovered loveys. Since the original Blankie had been a gift from one of Matt's work colleagues, I scoured the Internet in search of a replacement. I found a duplicate and eagerly clicked "purchase" without even checking the price tag. A backup, I reasoned, was worth any price. Nonetheless, when the backup arrived a few days later, Jackson wanted nothing to do with it. This one looked different, felt different, smelled different, and even *tasted* different than the original. So into a box the backup went, never to be touched until Teddy was born three years later.

Despite the intense attachment that each of my sons feels for his respective Blankie, these Blankies are constantly getting lost. Given the number of times that one of the boys' Blankies has gone missing, you would think we would've learned our lesson. But, sadly, the Case of the Missing Blankie keeps happening, often at the most inopportune times.

One night, on the eve of a family vacation to Florida, Teddy's Blankie went missing. Already stressed and anxious about the packing to do and the last-minute work projects to finish, I raced around the house looking under couch cushions, behind toilets, and in the car once, twice, and then a third time.

With each minute that passed, the panic escalated. Sweat started beading on my forehead and I threw off my bulky sweatshirt, scurrying around in sweatpants and a tank top like a marathon runner in training.

Jackson helped me look for a while. But as the hands on the clock ticked farther and farther past bedtime, I read them a short story and tucked each of them in for the night, assuring Teddy that we would find Blankie before we left the next day.

Then for thirty-five more long and frustrating minutes, I raced around the house like a mad woman on the brink of a meltdown. For thirty-five minutes, sweat slid down my face, back, and between my breasts. For thirty-five minutes, I flipped over couch cushions, looked in closets, peered beneath beds, and sifted through dirty laundry until finally—*finally!*—the raggedy blue Blankie was found lying at the bottom of the freezer. The freezer!

When I returned Teddy's special Blankie to him and told him it was in the freezer (because, of course, through all of this he insisted he had no idea where it was), his only reply was, "Oh, yeah, I wanted it to be cold" with that how-could-you-not-understand-the-pleasure-of-a-cold-Blankie tone in his voice. He buried his face in it with sweet contentment and an obvious understanding. And the truth is, I could understand because just two minutes earlier, when I found his little ragtag lovey nestled in the bottom of the freezer, right next to the bag of frozen broccoli and a years-old frozen Danish, I too had buried my own face in it and nuzzled that little rag myself. And believe me, at that moment, his cold little Blankie felt just a little bit like the velvety touch of an angel.

Over the years we have found missing Blankies behind the toilet, under the back deck, in the dogs' crate, between the bed frame, in a pile of dirty laundry, under pillows, on top of the computer, in the garage, in the freezer, and—my personal favorite—on the floor of a gas station bathroom. I have driven hours out of the way to retrieve lost or forgotten Blankies and I have dug through garbage, more than once, in search of a missing Blankie.

Each time those little rags of love are found, I do a victory dance and celebrate. Like the prodigal son has come home, I rejoice in the miracle of its return. I breathe a sigh of relief and say a silent prayer of gratitude that this night will not be the night that one of my sons is separated from his much-loved Blankie. That tonight will not be filled with tears, that tonight will not be when he is forced to say good-bye to his best friend, that tonight will be filled with peaceful slumber and dreams of knights and pirates and spaceships and unicorns.

Each time one of the boy's mass of fraying threads is found, I say a silent prayer of thanks that, *for now*, I can forget that they are growing up too fast; that, *for now*, the bittersweet passage of time is a little heavier on saccharine innocence than tart reality; that, *for now*, I can hold on to the miracle of childhood for a little bit longer. Because as much as finding what was once lost feels like a miracle and an act of divine intervention, the real miracle isn't the lost and found Blankie; the real miracle is the miracle of childhood. It is the miracle of hope, innocence, and unconditional love all wrapped up into a Blankie, doll, or teddy bear. It is the miracle of eyes lit up with excitement over ice cream with sprinkles, twinkly

Christmas lights, spoonfuls of peanut butter, freshly baked cookies, and the perfect smooth seashell. It is the miracle of absolute joy found in simple pleasures like sticker books and wet kisses from puppies and tickles that never quit. It is the miracle of constant learning and growing and soaking up everything the world has to offer. It is the miracle of forgiveness that is as easy as "I'm-sorry" and a hug, and friendship that is as easy as "I like trucks and you like trucks, so let's be friends."

For so much of my kids' lives, I have been eager to move on—for them to be walking, to be talking, to be out of diapers, for the tantrums to end. And now I'm finding that I'm happy just to linger here in this season and swim in the miracle of childhood for a while.

Enjoy it, it goes so fast. As much as on-the-eve-of-vacation searches for missing Blankies, tantrums in the dairy aisle at Jewel, and battles over homework are neither enjoyable nor fast, I know there will soon come a time when homework will be done behind locked bedroom doors, grocery shopping will be done alone, and Blankies will be tucked into boxes in the back of a closet. And I'm absolutely certain that, as I slowly amble through the quiet grocery aisles alone, a little piece of me will mourn this magical and miraculous time, this wondrous season of childhood.

There will come a time when my sons will pack their things and leave this house of lost Blankies and lost teeth, of first steps and first dates, of angry tears and forgiving hugs, of bitter disappointments and sweet successes. They will box up school pictures and class yearbooks, soccer trophies and sports jerseys, stuffed animals and their Blankies. And once they are gone, their rooms quiet and still, with a vague scent of the young boys who used to live there, I will pull out those raggedy old Blankies. I will snuggle them close, keep them safe, and pray that they never go missing again. Because from that point on, I will be the one who cannot sleep without those tattered Blankies, those soft and warm rags of love.

On Bended Knee

"Prayer is not asking. It is a longing of the soul. It is
daily admission of one's weakness. It is better in
prayer to have a heart without words than
words without a heart."
—Mahatma Gandhi

I did not come easily to prayer. Or, rather, this thing that
some people might refer to as prayer because, some days, I'm still
not sure if I'm doing it right.

As a child, I recited prayers—the Lord's Prayer, Hail Mary,
a family prayer before dinner—but they were scripted and
rehearsed. As we were growing up in a Catholic faith community,
my mother would sometimes take us to say the rosary during Holy
Week. In church each Sunday I would follow along with the order
of worship, saying the response prayers along with the rest of the
congregation.

I suppose that by some definitions those might be called
prayers, but I'm not sure that reciting scripted words can be called
prayers any more than calling up Domino's or picking up Thai on
the way home from work can be called cooking. There can be
spiritual nourishment from the recitation of ritual prayers, of
course, just like there is physical nourishment from Domino's pizza
and carryout Thai, but it's not the heart-calling kind of
communication with God, the Spirit, or the universe that prayer is
really all about.

Over the years, prayer started to become a little more
personal and less scripted for me, even though I'm not sure I knew

that my desperate callings and quiet pleas were actually prayers at the time. In high school, there were the angry prayers that my parents would just get a clue. There were the desperate what-do-I-do prayers and the unspoken prayers for love or confidence or wisdom. Sometimes prayer sounded a lot like screaming and yelling, nothing like the poetic prayers of meditation manuals or scripture; other times, the prayers came out as sighs and looked a lot like tears.

Prayer is a tricky thing for many of us, regardless of faith or religion. Of course, that doesn't stop us from throwing prayer around like a dish towel to sop up any messes about. "You're in my prayers," we say to the co-worker whose mother is in hospice. "I'm praying it all works out," we tell our neighbor while he waits to hear if he got the job. And there is the old saying that everyone is religious on Sunday, given all the prayers for football team wins traveling through the cosmos.

But what does that even mean? What is prayer and what does it mean to pray? And, perhaps more importantly, what happens when we pray?

Prayer, I think, is more than poetic words or distressed pleas to God. Prayer is an act of acknowledgement, acceptance, surrender, and empowerment all combined. As Marianne Williamson wrote in *Everyday Grace*, "When we pray to something higher than ourselves, we are not praying to something outside ourselves."[39] When we pray, we are acknowledging our hopes, dreams, and fears with honesty and vulnerability, accepting that certain things are outside of our control, surrendering ourselves to what is and what will be, and empowering ourselves to live with grace.

---

[39] Marianne Williamson, *Everyday Grace: Having Hope, Finding Forgiveness, and Making Miracles*, (New York: Riverhead Books, 2002), 31.

Over the years, I have learned that prayer isn't so much about the words that are said, or whether there are any words at all, as it is about intention, communication, and connection. Prayer is like tossing a fishing net into the deep abyss of our hearts, pulling out an ocean full of our deepest wants and needs—our lost and forgotten longings, our pretty hopes and tarnished regrets, our vibrant dreams and our translucently unrecognizable desires. Prayer is pulling out the net and setting it down on the beach, surrendering to what lies hidden inside the net, and then sifting through the weeds and the shells and the sea life, trying to make sense of it all. And prayer is using what we can from that tangled mess that we pulled out to change ourselves, to change the world, and to make something beautiful.

Sometimes I pray for my family and friends, calling out each of them by name, acknowledging the hopes I have for them. I don't expect that these prayers will change their circumstances or their fate, but I do expect that these prayers will change the way I will interact with them, perhaps bringing more empathy to our interactions or motivating me to reach out or offer help.

But the surprising thing I have realized recently is that most often my prayers consist of only one word: *please.* Just that one simple word, followed by a silence so loud it contains the whole depth of my heart. Maybe it's because I never really learned how to pray or maybe it's just because I'm lazy, but I think that God or the Spirit knows what follows that one simple word.

But what happens when we pray? Does prayer make any difference? Does it have any impact over the course of events, or the fate of our lives?

A few months ago, a friend of mine was dealing with a health scare for her child. There were lots of tests and conversations with doctors, plenty of worrying and speculation, and entirely way too much petrifying Internet information. There were very few answers or certainties. She was feeling scared, angry, and helpless. When we talked, the conversation turned to prayer.

"I can't even pray for him," she confessed. "I mean, why bother praying for him to be healed when I don't believe that's how it works. And there are enough people praying for him that *do* think that's how prayer works, so what's the point?"

"Maybe that isn't the purpose of prayer in the first place," I said. "Maybe the purpose of prayer isn't to change the situation, but to change our perception of the situation."

"Hmm . . ."

"Maybe in that sense, prayers *can* be answered. Maybe there is a releasing of the want or need or fear into the universe just by putting it out there and then letting it go. Maybe it's like dropping a coin in the fountain; it doesn't necessarily change fate, but it feels good just to put it out there and then release it a bit from our mental grip."

Maybe prayer isn't so much about words or requests as it is about the constant cycle of collecting and releasing, of grabbing hold and then letting go, of embracing and surrendering.

Prayer creates a humility bolstered by faith, a surrender inspired by confidence, and a passion tempered by mercy. I don't necessarily believe that prayer can change a situation, but I do think that it can change perceptions. A few months ago, I was feeling particularly dejected and uncertain about my writing career. I'd just received another rejection letter, my blog had been a bit stagnant, and I was suffering from a touch of writer's block. I seriously considered throwing in the towel on this book and giving up writing for good. I felt like I was spinning my wheels and stuck in limbo. And these feelings of rejection, insecurity, and confusion were affecting nearly every other aspect of my life. I was confused, agitated, and lost.

So I turned to prayer. I said a lot of *pleases* and waited. I asked for a sign, some way to know that the struggles were worth it. Prayer became a kind of therapy for me. The *pleases* turned into a mantra meditation; the questions became a therapy couch where I could lay it all on the line. In prayer, I admitted I was hurting, I acknowledged I had no idea what I was doing, and I asked for advice. A few days later, I got an e-mail from an old work acquaintance—a woman with whom I hadn't spoken in several years—telling me how much she enjoyed reading my blog posts. A few days after that, a high school acquaintance—a woman with whom I hadn't spoken in decades—reached out via Facebook to say that my words had touched her. Several weeks later, a stranger commented on one of my articles to say that it had helped her make peace with her family.

Some mystics and believers might call these "signs" or answered prayers, but really the situation hadn't changed at all. There was still no book deal (yet) for my manuscript, my blog readership was still stagnant, and I still had a serious case of writer's block. But despite the fact that the situation itself was entirely the same as it had been, my perception of the situation had completely changed. In prayer, I had become more attuned to the positive feedback I received instead of just taking in the negative feedback. In prayer, I became calmer and more patient. In prayer, I learned to open my eyes and ears, to pay attention to all that there was and not just what I wanted to see. In prayer, I was changed. As Soren Kierkegaard said, "The function of prayer is not to influence God, but rather to change the nature of the one who prays."

Learning to pray has been a long and slow process for me, and one that continues to change and evolve. Though I have come a long way in learning the *what* of prayer and the *why* of prayer, I am still figuring out the *how* of prayer, which like the other two is a wholly individual process.

Since I grew up in the Catholic church, kneeling and prayer seem to go hand in hand to me. Kneeling is not something that is done in the Unitarian Universalist church I attend (nor any other Unitarian Universalist churches that I am aware of), and I never realized how much I would miss the sacred act of kneeling. With head bowed, eyes closed, and knees pressed into holy ground, I'm able to surrender myself in prayer physically, mentally, and soulfully. Since kneeling isn't part of my weekly worship ritual, I am coming up with new *how's* of prayer. I pray while driving, while chopping vegetables for dinner, and while running on the treadmill. I pray for the little things—for the tantrum to end, for the traffic to move, for the energy to run one more mile. And I pray for the big things—for my children's happiness, for my husband's peace of mind, for health, for confidence and serenity. But these prayers are always fleeting. They come in fits and starts. They are authentic cries for help. They are purposeful expressions of gratitude, focused and one-dimensional. But they are generally one-way messages, not a two-way conversation.

These random, off-the-cuff prayers are essential to my spiritual well-being. But so are the all-consuming, soul-retching, rambling, hopeful, sorrowful, purposeful, aimless, holy conversions that I seem to be able to enter into only when I am engaged in the physical act of prayer. The physicality of mindful prayer (or meditation) is not unique to any one religion. In fact, people of many different faiths use the body to tap into the mind and soul. As Anne Lamott wrote in *Bird by Bird*, "Rituals are a good signal to your unconscious that it is time to kick in."[40]

So sometimes I sneak into my bedroom, quietly shut the door, crouch down next to my bed, and pray. I usually only have a few minutes before Jackson will need help with homework, or Teddy will need help in the bathroom, or my mind will start to wander, but those few minutes of prayer on bended knee are a precious miracle for me.

We need all types of prayers. We need the desperate, cry-for-help prayers and the hushed pleas for mercy. We need the therapy sessions and the jump-up-and-down, gratitude-laden exaltations. We need the rushed, frantic, off-the-cuff spontaneous

---

[40] Anne Lamott, *Bird by Bird: Some Instructions on Writing and Life*, (New York: Anchor Books, 1994), 117.

prayers and the head bowed, down-on-our-knees, whole-body prayers. We need them all.

And what I'm realizing as I begin to open my heart and mind to the concept of prayer is that the *what* of prayer, the *why* of prayer, and the *how* of prayer don't really matter all that much. It is the connection of the prayer, the internal peace and the growing closer of prayer, that are the true miracles.

The Road to Aurora

"Dogs are our link to paradise. They don't know
evil or jealousy or discontent. To sit with a dog on a
hillside on a glorious afternoon is to be back in
Eden, where doing nothing was not
boring—it was peace."
—Milan Kundera

The day before our first anniversary, Matt and I decided what we really needed were *dogs*. Because nothing says "Happy Anniversary, honey!" like two tiny fur balls that pee and poop in your house and chase each other around barking before the sun has come up, right? They say paper is the traditional first anniversary gift, but Matt and I opted for dogs instead. Huh.

The decision to get the dogs was rather impulsive so, naturally, it was at my prompting. The day before our anniversary we drove four hours north from Chicago to central Wisconsin to pick up our new puppies. Yes, plural.

While the impulsive decision to get a dog in the first place may have been mine, the decision to bring home two was Matt's.

"They can keep each other company," he reasoned.

I agreed, failing to see all of the errors in this faulty rationalization. In any event, we chose two puppies from the same litter, naming them Jobe and Maeby.

Jobe (pronounced like "Job" from the Bible, but named after G.O.B. from the television show *Arrested Development*) was skittish and cuddly, immediately climbing right into my lap. He shook when airplanes flew overhead and craved physical contact at all times.

His sister, Maeby (also named after a character from *Arrested Development*), was the yin to his yang. Where he was mostly white other than the black circles around his eyes, she was entirely black with the exception of a soft white underbelly. She was feisty to his gentle, bold to his meek, confident to his uneasy.

Despite their differences, both were boisterous, loud, and completely unmanageable. They awoke at four in the morning and chased each other around our small two-bedroom condo. They were so tiny at this age that they were able to get under our bed and tussle with each other throughout the early morning hours. Eventually, they started eating away at the bottom of our box spring until they had chewed a pretty good-sized hole in the underlining of the box spring, which then allowed them to engage in their early morning shenanigans not just under our bed but in the mattress itself.

Over the course of the next few months, they literally ate us out of house and home, chewing up more of our bed, the bottom of almost every piece of furniture, and even the walls. They drove us to the brink of madness. We had the very best of intentions, but absolutely no experience or sense whatsoever when it came to training and raising dogs. We took them to Puppy Boot Camp at the local pet store, but grew discouraged with the advice and instructions. Like picking food from the buffet line, we chose piecemeal training techniques that would work for us and ignored the ones that wouldn't, which, of course, was utterly ineffective.

For four months the puppies pooped, peed, and chewed on just about every surface in our small condo. Exasperated, Matt and I snapped at each other about what to do. Finally, after a few months we realized that as cute as Jobe and Maeby were, they were wreaking havoc on our home and our relationship. Something had to change.

Over the next few weeks, we armed ourselves with as much information as possible. We researched training techniques and we developed a plan. We bought a crate to help with house training, adjusted our morning and evening routines to allow for long walks, and hired a dog walker. Over the next several months, our two little fur balls of frenzy grew calmer and more manageable. They stopped chewing the walls and the bottom of the box spring (true, they may have just run out of box spring to chew, but it stopped all the same). They stopped relieving themselves in the house like it was their personal toilet (well, they relieved themselves less frequently, at least). They stopped running around like little tornadoes of mayhem. And over the next several months, Matt and I stopped keeping score about who was doing more, ceased beating ourselves up about how we were horrible dog owners, and stopped regretting our decision to get the dogs in the first place. We became a team, our own little pack.

Eventually our oh-my-gosh-what-did-we-get-ourselves-into exasperation turned into a what-would-we-do-without-the-dogs appreciation. Over the years, regular walks with Jobe and Maeby have carried me through some of the darkest days of my life—through multiple miscarriages, fertility problems, and disappointments so sharp I sometimes wondered how I would survive. Crawling into bed at night, exhausted and beaten and worn and not entirely sure I would be able to get up and do it all again in the morning, Maeby would curl up between my legs and Jobe would rest his chin on my back as if to say, "It's okay, you can rest now. We'll take care of you."

When we brought our sons home from the hospital, the dogs eyed them cautiously from a distance and tolerated stubby little fingers that grabbed fistfuls of fur. They pranced along on long walks through our northwest Chicago neighborhood, leashes held in one hand, and the stroller pushed with the other. They barked at strangers and other dogs, protecting our little clan. The dogs sat quietly at Matt's feet during meals, awaiting the treats of hamburger, chicken, or cheese that would inevitably come. They endured a move to the suburbs and countless long drives up to Wisconsin to visit my family. While we were away, they patiently awaited our return and rejoiced with a happiness that was almost electric when we walked through the door.

Until one fall day.

While playing fetch in the backyard, Maeby stopped in her tracks and didn't move for a few minutes. A visit to the vet the next morning revealed that she had essentially gone into cardiac arrest due to an excessive amount of fluid collecting around her heart.

"What causes this?" I asked the vet, certain that her explanation would be a mild and routine medical condition, but afraid that it could be something worse.

When she replied that it was likely caused by a tumor, I think my heart stopped beating momentarily and the earth spun slightly off its axis. After several tests and examinations, visits with veterinary specialists and one incredibly expensive surgery to have her pericardium removed, we were told Maeby did, in fact, have cancer. Without treatment, our small but spunky Maeby would likely die within a month. With chemotherapy, at only five years of age, she might have a 10 percent chance of making it one more year.

"I just want one more summer with her," Matt said desperately. "I just want her to have one more chance to run in the backyard and chase the ball."

I know he didn't really mean this. He wanted so much more than a year, so much more than a few more months to play fetch with Maeby, his first and only little girl.

As did I.

I could say that we weighed the pros and cons about whether to undergo the surgery and chemotherapy, but really there was no decision to make. We would do whatever it took to save

Maeby. We were not ready to say good-bye. We were not ready to resign ourselves to the loss and grief that would eventually come.

Of course, there are people who thought (or maybe even said), "Why would you go to all that time and hassle and expense? It's *just* a pet. It's not like it's a person." True enough. A dog is not a person. Dealing with a pet's health problems (and eventual mortality) is not the same as dealing with a child's illness or a parent's death. Of course not. But make no mistake about it, a pet is never *just* a pet either.

So the decision was made, and thus began our monthly journeys to Aurora, a suburb of Chicago about an hour southwest of where we live. Every month I would drop off Jackson and Teddy at my mother-in-law's house for the afternoon, say good-bye to Jobe as he scratched and whined at the door, and let Maeby ride shotgun in the front seat.

As time-consuming and inconvenient as the rides to Aurora were over the course of those months of chemo treatments and check-ups, in a way they were also therapeutic. The task of coordinating vet appointments, making childcare arrangements, and enduring the long drives gave me something to do and diverted my mind from the bigger fears and uncertainties. The doing kept me from the thinking. And in that, it saved me. Because thinking too much tended to bring me back to the same bitter thought: *Why? What have we done to deserve this?* To which the answer was always an angry, *We DON'T deserve this.*

We are hard-working, nice people. We pay our taxes, we go to church, and we donate to charity. We get up in the morning, pushing aside the exhaustion and the lost dreams and the doubts. We pour cereal for our kids and deal with tantrums and read *Green Eggs and Ham* fifteen times a day. We shower and go to work. We deal with snippy clients and demanding bosses. We pay our bills, make dinners, and send birthday cards. We say, "I love you" and "I'm sorry." Sure we fight, but then we forgive. Sure we make mistakes, but for the most part we are decent people, and kind people. We follow this path and do the "right" things. We tell ourselves that we do things because they are the good and kind things to do, but deep down if we are really being honest, we hope that by doing the right things and by being good that we will be insulated from the bad.

If we are kind and brave, amazing things will happen. I believe this to be true with all of my heart. But the opposite is not true. Being kind and brave does not prevent bad, horrible, heartbreaking things from happening. Bad things happen to good people. There is no karmic insurance policy to protect against that brutal side of life, like cancer and car accidents and depression and addiction. This cycle of entitlement (or lack thereof) that measures worth and justification only puts up walls and dividing lines.

As a Unitarian Universalist, I believe in the inherent worth and dignity of all beings. With this as one of my guiding principles, there can be no entitlement, no sense of just desserts. As humans, we are all flawed and imperfect; we are all unique and full of beauty. No one—absolutely no one—"deserves" to suffer from cancer, mental illness, or addiction. Yet when we begin to say, "*I* don't deserve this," we are in some small way saying that someone else does.

Connection—sacred connection—comes from a sense of togetherness in this slushy stew of life. There are no guarantees, there is no "right" path, no way to insulate ourselves from grief, sadness, and struggle. But this is also the essence of the shared human experience, and what breaks down walls, opens boxes, and binds us together.

Nearly four years later, after several rounds of chemo injections and chemo pills, Maeby is effectively cured. As they like to say in the veterinary oncology circles, she "shows no signs of cancer." In the words of her cancer doctor, she is a "canine anomaly."

To me, however, she is nothing short of miracle. This story could have so easily played out differently, and so often the story does turn out differently. As could all of our stories.

We do the best we can, and we do kind and brave things, but we don't do them to insulate ourselves from the pain or to earn a guarantee that bad things won't happen. We do kind and brave things the best that we can. We go to work, pay our bills, cook dinner for our kids, and fall into bed at the end of the day only to get up the next morning to do it all over again, because that is what we *can* do and *need* to do. We don't do it as part of some cosmic insurance policy, but because that is what we are called to do. Sometimes things don't turn out as we would like. Sometimes really horrible, painful, makes-no-sense things happen. All we can do is cling to each other, pray a little, and string together the cords of misery and despair to any threads of hope and renewal that we can find.

Sometimes really wonderful, happy, makes-no-sense things happen. And then, too, we cling to each other, pray a little, and string together the knotted threads. We rejoice and we celebrate.

ABCs and 1-2-3's

"It is not that I'm so smart. But I stay with the
questions much longer."
—Albert Einstein

When Jackson was learning to read, he was easily
frustrated, as was I. Sometimes he seemed eager and ready to learn,
sounding out words and trying to spell words often used in his
lexicon. Words like *zoo* and *hippo* and *veterinarian*. He would struggle
for a little while, get quickly frustrated, and then scream, "Just tell
me!"

Most of my attempts to teach him to read ended in
slammed doors (him) and cursing (me) and a flurry of tears (both
of us). Needless to say, I was pretty sure he wouldn't be reading in
kindergarten. In fact, given his frustration and reluctance to learn
most days, I lowered the bar considerably and decided that if he
learned to read before puberty, I would be happy.

And then one day, while I was helping in his kindergarten
classroom, I realized that—*ohmygosh!*—he could actually read a few
words. Not many, but enough to make it through a few pages of a
Dick and Jane book or *Green Eggs and Ham*. A few months later, he
was reading street signs and labels in the grocery store. A few
months after that, Matt and I learned the hard way that we could
no longer spell cuss words or adult secrets. The following year, in
first grade, he started bringing home books with smaller print and
fewer pictures. Then one morning, I came upstairs to find him
reading a book—a chapter book, no less—to Teddy.

It's a miracle! Somewhere, somehow, he had learned to read
and was continuing to learn to read. When did this happen? How

did he go from a crying baby who never slept to a walking and talking toddler, and then a running preschooler, and now a reading first grader? How did all of this happen?

"It is a miracle!" I wanted to shout from the rooftops. "My son knows how to read! Do you have any idea how amazing that is?"

And the truth is: it *is* amazing and it *is* a miracle. Not just that a child can read, but that we—children and adults alike—learn and grow, that we can question and find answers, that we can teach and be taught. And in doing so, we keep adding links to the chain of connection.

I would like to be able to take responsibility for his literacy, but it is largely due to some phenomenal teachers—these amazing and patient geniuses who have somehow figured out how to transform frustrated and reluctant little children into eager and excited learners. Teaching, sadly, is not something that comes easily to me (in fact, a tutoring session with a high school boyfriend may or may not have ended with pencils thrown across the room in anger and frustration), making me all the more appreciative for the miracles teachers perform every day. Miracles such as teaching children to read, doing long division, and naming the US presidents; helping children tie their shoes, shoot a basketball through the hoop, and make new friends.

And I am so grateful for all of the teachers—both in school and in life—who molded and shaped my own life. For Ms. Hansen, the high school art teacher who taught me how to do calligraphy, make pottery, and feed my soul through art, creativity, and imagination. For Mr. Knoke, the high school history teacher who taught me about the law and politics and justice. For my parents, who taught me—and continue to teach me—about generosity, community service, and faith. For Pastors Jen and Dave, who taught me about faith, spirituality, and God's transformative powers. For Matt, who taught me how to feel beautiful and how to be a family. For Jackson and Teddy, who taught me patience and unconditional love.

There are teachers everywhere, if only we are willing to be taught. It is hard, so very hard, to learn something new, whether walking, talking, reading, or new math; whether it's a new yoga pose, a new language, or a new point of view; whether it's how to make a soufflé, understand web code, or talk to our crazy uncle without coming unhinged.

Whether it's how to grow vegetables, hem a pair of pants, or be a better listener, learning is hard, tedious, and uncomfortable work. Learning takes a patient teacher and a willing student. It takes time and effort, failure and starting again. Learning new things is so hard that it's no wonder our learning curves tend to taper off the older we get.

But how strange is it that despite the fact that we expect young children to learn difficult and intimidating skills, like reading and shoe tying, we let our own life education fade. We get stuck and say, "This is enough." We tell ourselves that learning is something best left to children. We rationalize that we already know everything we need to know. We reason that we don't have the time or energy. We are slow to learn new activities or understand different viewpoints. We get stuck in a faith or culture or career that doesn't meet our needs or feed our soul because exploring something new is just too uncomfortable or time-consuming. We take the just-tell-me approach instead of sifting through sticky issues about faith and spirituality, politics and religion, relationships and personalities.

But when we stop learning and growing, we stop connecting. The chains of connection between the teacher and the student, between people and ideas and resolutions, with ourselves and with the Spirit, are severed when we stop learning. And we're all just a little bit worse off because of it.

So my mantra is simple: Never stop learning.

Read, converse, debate. Because learning isn't found in knowing things, but in understanding them. Learning isn't found on soapboxes; it's found in deep listening and respectful information sharing. It isn't found just in the memorization of facts, but in learning people and emotions and personalities, in learning what makes you feel good and bad and where your heart is called. Learning isn't surrounding ourselves with people who look like us, talk like us, think like us, and act like us; learning is found in accepting differences and building bridges.

Don't ever stop learning. Ask questions, wonder, and then ask some more questions. Because learning isn't found in timed tests, SAT scores, or rudimentary assessments. It's found in the questions without easy answers and the questions that have no answers at all. Learning isn't found in the just-tell-me's, but in the I-don't know's and the let's-figure-it-out's. It isn't found in evaluations, standards, and measurements; it's found in curiosity, skepticism, and an unquenchable sense of awe. Learning isn't found on the well-worn path, but the path overgrown with moss and vines waiting to be explored.

Don't ever stop learning. Try, fail, and try again. Because learning isn't found in the easy successes; it's found in the hard-fought failures and the second chances and the skinned knees. It's found in what happens after the missed shot at the buzzer, in the rejection letters, and in the red pen edits. Learning isn't found in getting the first job, but through interview after interview after interview; it isn't found in the easy A, but the hard-earned B minus.

Don't ever stop learning. And, for that matter, don't ever stop teaching either. Learning and teaching, after all, are one of the truest forms of connection there ever was.

Love in the Library

*"After all these years, I see that I was mistaken
about Eve in the beginning; it is better to live
outside the Garden with her than inside
it without her."*
—Mark Twain

Looking back, I have to say that I had no idea Halloween 1999 would be the night that changed everything. When I walked down the stairs into the subterranean bar, filled with ghouls and goblins, witches and devils, skeletons and superheroes, I had planned to have a couple of quick drinks and then head home. I was tired and not really in the mood for partying, let alone dealing with the throngs of people out for one of the biggest parties of the year.

Once we were finally inside, I began the slow dance of weaving my way through the crowd to reach the bar for a drink. I felt inadequate in my lame Halloween costume—an old prom dress, plastic tiara, and sash that read "Miss Halloween"—and was really just counting down the minutes until it was late enough that I could excuse myself and head home.

Eventually, I reached the bar and grabbed the attention of one of the bartenders to order Cosmopolitans for my friends and me. I paid the bartender, applied a fresh coat of lipstick, adjusted the bustier on my costume, and turned around to make my way back toward my friends.

But when I turned around I bumped into a guy from the law school I was attending. We had most of our classes together and were in the same study group (where, truthfully, we gossiped a lot more about other law school students and discussed the latest articles in my *Glamour* magazine than we did torts or contracts), but we weren't necessarily good friends.

"Hey!" he yelled to me over the loud music. "How are you?"

"Fine," I mumbled, feeling even more insecure about my lame costume and horrible makeup. "How are you? Who are you here with, anyone from school?"

"No, just a bunch of buddies from back home. They couldn't pass up Halloween in Madison."

"Yeah, that's for sure." My eyes glanced around, searching for my friends. I knew I should try to find them—I had their drinks after all—but, for some reason, I couldn't move, and it wasn't just because I was physically barricaded by the mobs of partygoers surrounding me.

We talked for a few more minutes. He showed off his equally lame costume, told me about the friends who had traveled hours for the legendary Halloween parties in Madison, and laughed about a flirty girl who had painted glitter on his cheek. Eventually, my friends beckoned me to dance, and we played a few songs on the jukebox. But while I danced in the corner, I kept glancing in his direction out of the corner of my eye.

My friends and I left shortly thereafter, and as we walked to our car, this unsettled feeling took over me—a strange mix of sadness, jitters, jealousy, and excitement. A few hours ago, that guy from law school study group had gone from "that guy" to That Guy, something I wasn't ready for, prepared for, or all that happy about for that matter.

A few days later, the two of us were in the back of the law school library, sitting in the chairs closest to the expansive windows looking out over Bascom Hill. Maybe it was the chance encounter a few days earlier or maybe it was the romantic nostalgia that's carried in on the cool air each fall, but for whatever reason, we couldn't seem to focus on the civil procedure midterm for which we were supposed to be studying. Civil procedure was, by far, the most complicated of first-year law school subjects for me to grasp, so I probably should have been trying to learn more about amorphous legal concepts like laches, affirmative defenses, and compulsory joinder, but I really just wanted to learn more about *him*. What did he think of our torts professor and that annoying girl who was always shooting her hand in the air? Where did he grow up? Did he have any siblings and what were they like? What did he think he would do next summer: get an internship, take some classes, find a job? Where had he gone to college and what brought him here to Wisconsin? Who were those crazy friends of his on Halloween night? How did he get that infectious laugh and (gasp!) did he have a girlfriend?

A few weeks later, That Guy bought me a blueberry muffin. A few days after that, we had our first official date, and within a few more days, I was pretty sure that That Guy was The One.

In some respects, finding Matt when I did was nothing short of a miracle. As it turns out, we had been living in the same town for a few years and although we had mutual friends in common, our paths didn't cross until we came to law school. We both had lives to live, certain life-changing experiences to go through, and things to work out within ourselves before we would be ready for each other. Had we met any sooner, things might not have worked out like they did. Had we met a little later, well, he could have ended up with that flirty girl in the bar on Halloween night.

Finding love at any time is kind of a miracle when you think about it. I'm not sure I believe in love at first sight or the idea of soul-mates, but I do know that anytime two people can come together and set off mutual sparks inside each other, anytime two people can go from two *me's* to a *we*, the result is pretty amazing.

But the real miracle isn't that Matt and I found each other or that we found each other when we did. The real miracle is the fact that we are still in love all these years later and that we made it through some really tough seasons together. The real miracle isn't the feeling of love, but the commitment of love.

There are so many things that can step into a marriage and rock the boat. Children, health problems, financial stress, moves, in-laws, and jobs all have a way of climbing into the boat, shifting the center of gravity, and making waves. And if the boat isn't heavy enough and your hands aren't gripping the sides, the boat can capsize or someone might go overboard.

I have seen too many marriages tip over and seen too many people fall out of the boat not to realize just how incredible it is to stay in the boat in the first place, let alone keep the boat moving steadily through the water with both spouses paddling.

Like any marriage, ours has gone through its fair share of harsh seasons. Seasons that were a little too heavy on keeping score and a little too light on appreciation, seasons filled with heartbreak and a kind of emptiness that neither of us could have imagined. There were a few seasons filled with resentments and lingering anger that spiraled and grew until we weren't even sure what we were upset about in the first place, and some seasons that rocked our boat fiercely, relentlessly, and dangerously. But the really amazing thing is that even when we were going through those harsh and bitter seasons, I was never really scared that our boat would tip over or that one of us would fall out. It was like there was a heavy anchor on the bottom of the boat, holding it in place, and we had seatbelts strapping us safely into the boat. We might get seasick, but we wouldn't fall out.

Fortunately, in the past ten years of marriage, the warm and calm seasons have outnumbered the harsh and bitter ones. Seasons filled with "thank you's" and sticky notes left on the nightstand, with date nights and hand-holding, with Friday night dance parties and Sunday night movies. Many seasons when problems seemed manageable and challenges seemed minor. And, fortunately, there have mostly been seasons when all of the waves outside of the boat seemed to be small, or at least moving in the same direction that the boat is.

The truth is, there are so many waves that splash up on the boat that is marriage. There are sweet seasons, and there are bitter ones, and sometimes all we can do is hold on and keep paddling. Heck, sometimes we can't even paddle; we just need to float and rest with each other for a little while. Finding love is always something to be celebrated; it is absolutely amazing to me that the universe will work out in such a way that two compatible people will be in the right place at the right time and a whole new life together can be created. Finding love, in the first place, is pretty awesome.

But it is the staying in love, the committing to love, the continually falling in love with each other day after day after day that is the real miracle in it all. If you are married, find that person now—whether he or she is at work, or in the kitchen washing dishes, or putting the children to bed—and say "I love you." Tell her you appreciate her. Tell him he is everything you could have hoped for and more. Look past the socks he left lying on the floor and ignore her nagging complaints about the socks you left lying on the floor. Thank him for making dinner, even if it is powdered macaroni and cheese from the box. Buy her those fancy cookies she likes just because you are thinking of her. Send him flirty e-mails. Ask her out on a date. Talk about something other than the kids and the depleted checking account. Dream about vacations you'll take together and tell each other something you haven't told anyone else. Say "I'm sorry" and mean it, even when you don't think you have anything to be sorry about.

Marriage isn't about dirty socks or honey-do lists or fancy dinners. Marriage is about thoughtfulness and appreciation and dreaming together. Marriage is about reaching out and holding on—to the marriage and to each other—especially when the waters get a little rocky and unsettled. Marriage is about sharing, committing, and connecting. Marriage is about finding a way to fall in love with each other again and again, even when you're so mad that you can't possibly imagine why you ever fell in love with this person in the first place.

Marriage isn't some romantic fairytale with a knight in shining armor or a princess in some castle; it is two flawed and imperfect people coming together to create something beautiful. Marriage isn't about creating a storybook happily ever after, but about creating a lifetime of everyday miracles.

Singing Your Song

"A bird doesn't sing because it has an answer, it sings because it has a song."
—Maya Angelou

This book, I think, has been growing in my head and in my heart for years. Maybe even my entire life, though the act of writing was a rather stunning surprise. I didn't set out in life to be a writer, but I have always been a bit of a grammar snob. As a child, I envisioned my adult life consisting of an office, dress pants, and manicured fingernails—for a while—and then crayons at the kitchen table, carpooling, and . . . manicured fingernails.

Strangely, my adult life did actually look like that for many years. Minus the manicured fingernails, of course. I lawyered in an office wearing dress pants. And then I left the legal world to be an at-home mom and spent my time coloring at the kitchen table and carpooled. I won't be all melodramatic and say I loved each of those roles, because the truth is I felt like there was this little piece of the puzzle missing in both roles.

I started writing slowly, in an almost desperate way. Through a series of chance encounters and strokes of luck, I found myself doing legal writing on a freelance basis for a handful of attorneys around the city. The work wasn't particularly challenging, nor was it all that stimulating, but I found the process of writing to be oddly satisfying. I enjoyed the process of fitting words together to form ideas that would, in some way, reach the intended reader. And as I spent more and more time writing web copy and newsletters about negligence, broker-dealer regulations, or immigration reform, I inadvertently seemed to be opening the cage of some animal that had been cooped up for thirty years.

Slowly, cautiously, and in timid whispers, I started to wonder if writing might actually be something I could do, something I might actually be good at.

And then I pushed that dream back in its cage for a while, and buried my head and my body in the daily tasks of running a household and raising a family. A writer? Me? *That's silly*, I thought. *What were you thinking?*

But late at night, and in those quiet moments of late afternoon, during long runs when my head cleared itself of the heavy tread of reality, the animal would push its head through the cage's bars. *A book*, it purred, *you should write a book.*

"Why don't you write a book?" Matt said as we lay in bed late one night.

I listed all of the reasons why I shouldn't write a book. Lack of time, money, energy, to name a few. But really my reasons for not writing boiled down to two things: a fear of not finding my voice, and a fear of not being any good.

But eventually the animal grew too big.

I started writing and I realized quickly that I couldn't stop. I wrote about my crisis of faith, about finding the Spirit at Second Unitarian Church, about religion and spirituality, and about losing faith and then finding it again. I wrote about love and family, about the mirage of perfection and the battle for balance, about despair and loss, and about hope and resilience.

As I wrote, the fear of not finding my voice quieted and calmed with a head pat and a hush. The more I wrote, the more I realized this voice had been there all along. Because we *all* have a voice, whether loud or quiet, talking in this language or that: it is the voice of the Spirit, uncaged.

Of writing, Shauna Niequiest says:

What writing teaches me, over and over, is that God is waiting to be found everywhere, in the darkest corners of our lives, the dead ends and bad neighborhoods we wake up in, and in the simplest, lightest, most singular and luminous moments . . . When I write, I find a whole new universe I never saw before, like being underwater for the first time, having never before seen what's under the glassy surface . . . We hide and we seek, and we lose ourselves in the best possible way, and find things around us and inside ourselves that we never expected.[41]

I have found that writing has cracked open this space inside me that had been hidden and closed. Like that junk drawer in the kitchen or the hallway closet, this space inside my soul was crammed to near bursting with resentments, doubts, hopes, dreams, ideas, and all that icky, scary stuff you don't want to deal with so you stuff it into the drawer or closet and pretend it's not there by pouring another glass of wine or eating another cookie.

Like a California Closets sales rep, the voice of the Spirit sweeps through and tidies up a bit. It helps us see that there is a place for all of this clutter, and there is an outlet for all of these feelings that we kept shoving down, down, down. For some of us, we find our voice while writing; others find it behind the camera, in the kitchen, or while teaching young children.

Of course, we all have a voice. The Spirit is in all of us. The difficult part is not just finding our voice, but using our voice, because that little rascal—fear—likes to tell our voice to "hush up" every now and then. Fear can be so loud and persuasive that whenever our voice is able to tell the fear to scram, it really is a

---

[41] Niequist, *Cold Tangerines*, 137.

miracle. A miracle that we found our voice, that we're using our voice, and that the voice of the Spirit is singing.

Find your voice, use your voice, and celebrate your voice. It is, in some ways and at some moments, the only thing we have, and the only thing that will connect.

Open Boxes and Knotted Threads

*"Our ancient experience confirms at every point
that everything is linked together,
everything is inseparable."*
—Dalai Lama XIV

In our hallway closet, there are still the flowered boxes that hold old photos and birthday cards, newspaper clippings, and school report cards. But now, below those pretty boxes, there also sits a beaten cardboard box. We use this box as our donation box, or connection box, if you will. We fill the box with unused purses and clothes that don't fit anymore, children's books that the boys have outgrown, and knick-knacks that are taking up space. Unlike the pretty boxes at the top of the closet—the ones that separate, package, and hide—this box is utilitarian, open, and exposed. It is indiscriminate in the contents that it holds, and nothing is off limits. A silk scarf might sit atop a Dr. Seuss book, a picture frame might lie next to some running shoes, a pair of earrings might be nestled inside a leather computer bag. There is no separation, only integration and, I hope, a kind of continuity and fluidity. Maybe even a thread of connection, with pieces of our home making their way into the homes of someone else and so on.

And while the pretty cartons at the top of the closet hold the memories of my life, this box—the big, functional, no-frills, wide-open one—is the way that I want to *live*. Big, fluid, purposeful, and open. Connecting, serving, and celebrating. And what I am finding is that with the right tools, with ropes and threads and needles, it is actually possible to turn a big and open cardboard box into something even more beautiful than the pretty boxes that line the top shelves of the closet.

I spent a lot of my life hiding from spirituality and strands of the Spirit, assuming that these things were best left for religious fanatics or mystic hippies. Like Benjamin Franklin said, "A place for everything, everything in its place." I put career in one box, family and friends in another. Spirituality was kept in the tiny box in the corner, where I could open it privately in church on Sunday mornings or during frantic middle-of-the-night prayers.

But a few years ago I grew tired of lugging around the heavy boxes that were separating the various pieces of my life—work, family, friends, spirituality. I was weary and exhausted; the weight was just too heavy, the questioning voices too loud. *Why do I feel so disconnected? Why is there all this separating and hiding? Isn't there some way to tie this all together?*

So I put down the boxes, lifted off the lids, and peeked inside. What I found inside those heavy boxes was both strangely foreign and surprising familiar. Inside those tightly bound crates were the gossamer strings of the Spirit.

There is a kind of desperate longing for spirituality in our everyday lives, a kind of magnetic force pulling us out of the faraway corners of ourselves. There seems to be this tiny voice calling to us: come, live, feel, connect.

I had heard this voice for a long time but paid little attention to it. The voice didn't really seem to be speaking my language, and I couldn't understand what it was saying. It was much easier to ignore the voice, put everything in its place, and close the lids.

But eventually all that separating, packaging, and hiding became more trouble than it was worth. The boxes were too heavy, the sorting was too tedious, and the questions were too loud.

Eventually I decided to ask: *What if there is another way? Why not listen to what the voice is saying?*

There is another way. There is the open boxes way, the tying threads way.

This open-boxes-and-tying-threads way hasn't answered all of the questions, to be sure, but it has made this much clear: whether we admit it or not, there is a common thread of spirituality running through everything and everyone. *Everything and everyone.* We might call it God or the Spirit, the golden rule or a higher power. We might find spiritual guidance through Jesus or Muhammad, the Buddha or the Dalai Lama. We might see it in science or sunsets or seashells. We might experience it when we practice yoga or meditation; we might feel it in the tears that leak out of the corners of our eyes when we make it to church; we might hear it in our children's giggles from the room next door. Me, I find it in all of these things and in all of these ways. I find sacred connection in grace and wonder. I live it through everyday miracles.

However we feel it, in whatever way we name it, and whether we even admit it or not, the threads of spirituality are within us, around us, and among us. The threads of spirituality are everywhere, connecting everything.

One of the biggest perils of writing is that you take your unique and very personal experiences and try to tell them as bravely, honestly, and kindly as possible, and then you lay them out on the page for close inspection in the hopes that someone, anyone, will find some ounce of universal truth or trace of relatability within them. As writers, we lay ourselves bare; we risk public humiliation for sake of connection, not just with the reader, but with ourselves as well. I hope that these stories have given you a glimpse of the way that grace opens boxes and the ways that wonder creates space for the tied threads to climb out. I hope that these stories have given you a taste of the miracles that surround us each and every day. I hope that they have inspired you to find the

241

ways that you can find the grace, wonder, and everyday miracles in your own life. And I hope that the stories were filled with just enough universal truth to make them relatable. But I also hope that they have left open enough space for you to find your own truth as well.

To live fully and connect deeply means different things for different people. There is no firm definition, no mathematical equation, no rulebook. I can't tell you what living fully and connecting deeply means for you; I can only tell you what it means to me. It means grace and wonder and miracles.

I still don't know the answers to a lot of life's big questions. I don't know where we came from, where we are going, or what the meaning of all *this* is. But what I do know is that life— while far from easy—is a celebration filled with tiny moments of spectacular goodness. I also know that open boxes are a whole lot lighter, and that threads of connection—*sacred connection*—make the journey more tolerable, purposeful, and enjoyable. I know that having tasted the life of open boxes and tied threads, I don't want to go back to the way of closed packages and locked lids. I want a life that breathes and bubbles, makes me laugh and cry and stare with wide eyes, leaves me breathless and sweaty and grateful. *Don't you?*

If you do (and since you've read this far, I have a feeling that you do), let's do this. Together.

Let's open boxes and tie threads. Don't save anything for the other side; leave it *all* on the table. Seek out grace, stand back in wonder, and throw your hands up with giddy delight at the everyday miracles.

Live fully and connect deeply. That is my wish for you, for all of us.

Acknowledgements

When one gets to the end of a journey such as this, the words "thank you" somehow just don't seem like enough. Yet they are the only words that seem appropriate as well. So I will trust that the following people know that these two little words—*thank you*—hold every ounce of love, gratitude, and respect that I can stuff into them:

To the entire 220 Publishing team, especially Glenn, Stephanie, and Vania, for taking a chance on a relatively unknown writer, for your confidence in me, and for holding my hand as, together, we worked to bring my dream to fruition.

To Mary Kay Sergo for your unwavering faith, optimism, and support. And for introducing me to Glenn.

To my superb editors—Christy Scannell and Nicole Okerblad—for your expert eyes, constructive criticism, and for buoying me with your grace through what is, undoubtedly, a painstakingly difficult part of the writing process.

To Caroline Sass Blustin, Terra Westhaus, Kelly Jones, Angie McMonigal, and Matthew Organ for your time spent reading first drafts and second drafts and third drafts, your patience as I blabbered on about little details, and your kind feedback that, while constructive, never really felt like criticism.

To the Spirituality Girls—Elizabeth, Rachel, Leah, and Julie—who embody the true meaning of connection, hospitality, and community; to David and Jennifer Owen-O'Quill for your spiritual guidance; to Lisa Todd for being the first one to greet us when Matt and I walked into the Second Unitarian Church that early spring morning all those years ago; and to the folks at Countryside Church Unitarian Universalist for welcoming us into your spiritual home, not just once but twice.

To Michelle DeRusha and Margaret Placentra Johnston for your advice, support, and mentoring as I wend and weave my way through the publishing maze.

To my blog readers for your encouragement, support, and friendship; and to my fellow writers for your camaraderie, inspiration, and sense of community.

To Angie McMonigal for your gorgeous photographic images, some of which provided the inspiration for the beginnings of this book.

To my friends—especially Kelly Jones and Terra Westhaus—for the past twenty to thirty years of friendship; for your love and support; for your hand-holding, tear-wiping, and butt-kicking, depending on which one was needed when; for celebrating with me and crying with me; and for being there through it all.

To my Chicago in-laws, Ruth and Tom Organ, for watching Jackson and Teddy so that I could tap out the words of this book; and Mike and Sara Organ, for knowing me well enough to know that the best way to celebrate is with a ginormous cookie.

To my parents, Phil and Beth Sass, for teaching me the importance of faith, for your infinite generosity, and for the illogical amount of confidence you have in me.

To my sister, Caroline Sass Blustin, for sharing a room with me light-years ago and to her husband, Mike, for sharing a room with her now; and to my brother, Al Sass, for spending so many Saturday nights with me light-years ago, and to his wife, Heather, for spending Saturday nights with him now.

To Jackson and Teddy for continuously teaching me about grace and wonder, love and laughter, faith and forgiveness.

To Matthew for . . . well . . . *everything*. For your faith in this book and in me; for your patience, selflessness, and strength; for inviting me to be my best self; for buying me a blueberry muffin that cold November morning; and for being my partner in crime ever since then.